Remembering Silme Domingo and Gene Viernes

Remembering Silme Domingo and Gene Viernes

THE LEGACY OF FILIPINO AMERICAN LABOR ACTIVISM

RON CHEW

Published by the

ALASKERO FOUNDATION
Seattle

in association with

UNIVERSITY OF WASHINGTON PRESS
Seattle and London

UNIVERSITY OF WASHINGTON PRESS
PO Box 50096, Seattle, WA 98145, USA
www.washington.edu/uwpress

The inspiration for the design of this book came
from the *1952 Yearbook* of the International
Longshoremen's and Warehousemen's Union, Local
37, edited by Filipino American author, poet, and
migrant laborer Carlos Bulosan. The typefaces used
are Bodoni Highlight ICG, Brush Script Std, Adobe
Caslon Pro, Euro Bodoni T, Futura T, Poster Bodoni
BT, and Trade Gothic.

**LIBRARY OF CONGRESS
CATALOGING-IN-PUBLICATION DATA**
Chew, Ron.
Remembering Silme Domingo and Gene Viernes :
the legacy of Filipino American labor activism / Ron
Chew.
   p. cm.
Includes bibliographical references.
ISBN 978-0-295-99190-0 (pbk. : alk. paper)
1. Domingo, Silme, d. 1981. 2. Viernes, Gene, d.
1981. 3. Labor leaders—Washington (State) 4.
Minority labor union members—Washington (State)
5. Filipino Americans—Washington (State) 6.
Cannery workers—Labor unions—Pacific States. 7.
Asian Americans—Employment—Pacific States. 8.
Labor movement—Pacific States—History. I. Title.
HD6517.W2.C44 2012
331.88092'299210797—dc23   2011050253

The paper used in this publication is acid-free and
meets the minimum requirements of American
National Standard for Information Sciences—
Permanence of Paper for Printed Library Materials,
ANSI Z39.48<N>1984.∞

CONTENTS

ACKNOWLEDGMENTS

I'm grateful to the Inlandboatmen's Union (IBU), Region 37, for help in bringing this book project to life. I thank Terri Mast, national secretary of the IBU, for her vision, guidance, and leadership, and staff members Rich Gurtiza and John Foz, who helped me connect to documents and key interview subjects. I thank the International Longshore and Warehouse Union Local 37 Building Fund for providing the financial support to make this book possible.

I thank my very talented and resourceful partners at Chew Communications; their collaborative attitude and relentless focus made it possible to complete the project in fourteen months. My team consisted of Ed Echtle, chief researcher and photographer; Debbie Louie, layout artist and oral history transcriber; and Shannon Gee and Pei Ju Chou, the videographers who filmed the oral histories in this book. All were involved in various aspects of editing and shaping the format and final content of this book. As a producer at the Seattle Channel, Shannon served as the vital link between this book project and a companion film project at the Seattle Cable TV Channel. Thanks to the staff at the Seattle Channel for their support.

At the heart of this project are the stories of the Domingo and Viernes families and the activists who fought for progressive social change in the salmon canning industry. Full interviews were conducted with Abraham "Rami" Arditi, Emma Catague, David Della, Kalayaan Domingo, Ligaya Domingo, Lynn Domingo, Angel Doniego, Dick Farinas, John Foz, Rich Gurtiza, John Hatten, Julia Laranang, Terri Mast, Chris Mensalvas, Jr., Bruce Occena, Andy Pascua, Alonzo Suson, Emily Van Bronkhorst, Velma Veloria, Conan Viernes, Stan Viernes, Steve Viernes, and Michael Woo. I thank them for their thoughtfulness, candor, and lifelong commitment to equality and social justice. Excerpts from their interviews are featured here, but the full interviews have been transcribed and preserved in digital form. All the interview materials—and additional letters, documents, and photographs gathered in the course of this project—have been donated to the archives of the Wing Luke Museum in Seattle. Thanks to Bob Fisher and the staff at the museum for their support.

I am grateful to Andy Pascua and Steve Viernes for hosting me in Wapato and allowing me to reach deep into that community for information and images. I thank Dean Wong, the preeminent documentary photographer in the International District for nearly four decades, for stepping in at the last minute to capture photographs for the cover and some inside pages.

I thank Pat Soden, Marilyn Trueblood, Thomas Eykemans, and Laura Iwasaki at the University of Washington Press for their wise counsel and practical assistance; James N. Gregory, Harry Bridges Endowed Chair of Labor Studies at the University of Washington, for his work maintaining the Seattle Civil Rights and Labor History Project; the *International Examiner* for photographs; and Jodee Fenton, managing librarian of Special Collections at the Seattle Public Library.

I thank my sons, Cian and Kino, for tolerating my inattentiveness during many of the hours I spent working on this book.

I thank Gene Viernes and Silme Domingo for their indomitable spirit. This book is created in their memory.

Finally, I thank the many activists—especially those born after Silme and Gene—for continuing to work toward a society free of discrimination, poverty, and injustice. They create hope in this world.

Ron Chew
Seattle, Washington

PART **1**

The Era

"Not everything that is faced can be changed. But nothing can be changed until it is faced."

—James Baldwin

One Generation's Time
Thirty Years after the Domingo-Viernes Murders

By RON CHEW

A Personal Prologue

On June 1, 1981, Silme Domingo and Gene Viernes, two young Filipino American officers in Seattle's Local 37 of the International Longshoremen's and Warehousemen's Union (ILWU), were gunned down at their union hall in Pioneer Square. Today, the masonry structure, built in 1900, is a boarded-up remnant of a bygone labor era, waiting for the wide arc of the wrecking ball.

I had the privilege and the curse of knowing Silme Domingo and Gene Viernes well. They and a circle of community activists who grew to adulthood together in the 1960s and 1970s started their careers during this time of fierce idealism, radical politics, and boundless optimism. The era propelled many of them—many of *us*—into professions in nonprofit community service and social-change advocacy. But Silme and Gene never made it through to the

other side. Both were only twenty-nine at the time of their deaths. The horror of experiencing the murders when we were too young to deal with the deaths of peers left many of us struggling to heal and diverted much of our youthful energy into coping with the aftermath. We were blessed to know them, and yet we were cursed.

We share the stark memory of the exact moment when we heard that Gene and Silme had been gunned down. Over the years, when a memory of Gene's or Silme's voice, gesture, laughter, or expression flares out of nowhere, it is evident that the wounds have never quite healed over. Healing happens at its own pace and lives in a private spot that not even the closest of friends can enter.

Silme Domingo, a native of Texas, was raised in the predominantly white Ballard area of north Seattle but found his natural voice and passion in the tumultuous inner-city neighborhoods of Beacon Hill and the International District, where he hung out. Gene Viernes was raised in the small, tight-knit farming community of Wapato in Central Washington but found the breathing room to speak his mind when he came to Seattle, looking to create a political home for himself.

Silme and Gene were Alaskeros—Filipino Americans who worked in the Alaskan canneries—following in the path of their fathers. They spent summers in Alaska doing low-paying, dangerous jobs, cutting and

Former ILWU hall at Second Avenue and Main Street, Seattle.
Ed Echtle photo.

Silme Domingo in his Monte Carlo, ca. 1970s.
University of Washington Libraries, Special Collections, CWFLU Local 7 Papers.

packing fish on assembly lines like thousands of other Asian immigrants who had come before them.

In the early 1970s, the city boy and the country boy met after working several seasons in the cold, wet fish houses of Alaska. Their commitment to fighting the racial discrimination they witnessed and to building a new movement for workers' rights drew them together as allies. Silme, his older brother Nemesio Jr., Gene and other young workers were at the forefront of three class action discrimination lawsuits launched on behalf of thousands of Asian American and Native American cannery workers in 1973 and a gritty campaign to reclaim their union.

Gene and Silme were murdered at the peak of these efforts. In the aftermath, tireless investigation by family, friends, and political allies showed that they were the victims of an intricate conspiracy involving the corrupt president of ILWU Local 37 Tony Baruso and agents tied to Philippine dictator Ferdinand Marcos. In multiple trials during the ten years following the murders, four men went to prison for their role in the shootings, and courts ordered the Marcoses to pay restitution for their connection to the murders.

The lengthy search for justice and the charismatic presence of Silme and Gene in the Asian American movement and the drive for union reform make the exercise of looking back remarkably complex. Where does the story begin, and where does it end? Beyond the outsized images of martyred heroes created by the protracted and sensational media coverage, who were these young men, Silme Domingo and Gene Viernes? Who were Silme and Gene in the contexts of their coworkers, the generation they represented and the community they sought to serve?

It's dangerously myopic to allow a pair of murders to define a complex movement that includes many other activists of equal weight whose lives weren't ended prematurely. And those who die become caricatures of what they were in real life—idealized, simplified, or stereotyped in a way that cheats us of the opportunity to see them in human, correctly measured terms.

Bruce Occena, a fellow activist and close political ally of the two men, said he doesn't

Hong Kong Restaurant postcard. Cocktails were served in the Sampan Room.
Ron Chew collection.

see the two as "heroes." That, he said, was a "posthumous" descriptor. If they were still alive today, we would see them with "all of their warts and shortcomings," like the rest of us. "We do some things good and some things we still don't do good. They would be like that."

Silme and Gene were not so different from many of us who chose to work in the community and advocate for social justice. During the 1960s and 1970s, most of us wanted to change the world, a world that still treated our immigrant parents and people of color like second-class citizens. We wanted America to live up to its democratic ideals. Most of us shared this passionate desire, but each of us expressed it and fought for it in our own way, sometimes effectively, sometimes clumsily. What can be said about Silme and Gene is that both demonstrated an extraordinary level of commitment to their cause, both were natural leaders from a young age, and both were unyielding in their devotion to family, friends, and their community.

But we lost them before they realized their full promise. Now we're imprisoned in an echo

chamber of memories, trying to see and understand clearly only a brief chapter of the past. It's wearying to be ensnared inside an endless guessing game of what-ifs, rather than looking forward to what might still be.

I was the editor of the *International Examiner* in the late 1970s, when the newspaper was published by the Alaska Cannery Workers Association (ACWA), an advocacy group Silme, Nemesio Jr., and others had created for the purpose of pursuing legal action against the cannery companies in Alaska. For four years, I worked day and night alongside Silme and Gene in the dark unheated ACWA office in the International District. I had the privilege of knowing them as coworkers and friends.

I first noticed Silme from a distance. He and a boisterous group of Asian friends frequented the Hong Kong Restaurant, where I worked as a busboy, to eat and then drink in a cocktail lounge called the Sampan Room. Later, I met him up close at the Alaska Cannery Workers Association office. He would park his big burgundy Monte Carlo outside and stride into the office in his leather jacket, bell-bottom slacks, and platform shoes, full of life and humor, confident, almost cocky. Silme was a charmer, a naturally gifted networker, a fiercely committed activist who wore down opponents like a skilled courtroom attorney, with argument piled on top of argument during the course of community meetings that dragged on into the evenings.

Silme was stubborn and argumentative, but he also had the humility to admit when he went too far. Once, while we were discussing the *International Examiner*, he confessed that as both an editor and a contributor to the *Asian Family Affair* (another Asian American publication), he had the gall to publish an interview with himself. It was raw ego, he said, laughing at his own impudence. He was always reflective, trying to learn from his mistakes and grow as a person.

I met Gene a few years later. The "Wapato kid," he called himself. Other Seattle friends called him the "Filipino cowboy." He was a high-energy, unpretentious individual who never seemed quite at ease with the big-city pace of Seattle. In my mind's eye, I can still see Gene's bowlegged saunter, his torn jeans, the ubiquitous papers, books, and clipboard tucked under his arm, his deadpan humor, his mock Filipino accent, the way he would talk rapidly to hide his shyness, the way he chuckled instead of laughing, the way he would belch loudly for the "amusement" of the people around him.

Gene was a considerate friend. When he saw me working on stories for the *International Examiner* at night in the frigid office, he brought in a portable space heater and placed it by my feet. When he saw me distributing copies of the *Examiner* by myself, he would, in his macho style, grab a huge bundle in each arm on the pretense that he was "going down the street anyway" and then proceed

to take care of over half of the distribution.

Gene was the one I felt closest to. It may have been our mutual love of history, penchant for analyzing people from a distance, and similar working-class backgrounds or our equally wry, low-key personalities that drew us together. Whatever it was, it made for a sweet friendship. At the time of his death, I had been helping him with a book on the history of the Alaska canneries. Afterward, I couldn't continue because it was Gene's project more than it was mine, and he was no longer there to steer it into the final stage of writing. For years, the burden of grief was too great.

As different as Silme and Gene seemed to be, they were effective allies as community organizers, each bringing a different kind of intelligence to their work. Even though they often disagreed on political strategies or had different takes on the people around them, they found ways to work together. In any era and in any community, that's a monumental achievement for two young men endowed with headstrong personalities and more than an average dose of machismo.

Julia Laranang, a former ACWA staff member, said the stark differences between Gene and Silme not only made them a dynamic team; it also allowed them to knit together other activists who were also very dif-

Gene Viernes
Emily Van Bronkhorst collection.

Silme Domingo
John Foz photo.

ferent in personality and style. "This is really an example of where the whole was greater than the sum of the parts," she said. "They were able to achieve so much precisely because they were so different yet committed to fighting for the same cause."

In addition to organizing in the Alaska canneries, Silme and Gene were part of a wider movement of young activists and elderly residents working to restore the deteriorating hotels that made up the majority of the International District, the historic home of Asian immigrants in Seattle. In the 1970s, these buildings were still home to a community of immigrants and seniors but stood in the direct path of bulldozers that had arrived to make space for the Kingdome stadium and other large-scale public developments.

Silme and Gene participated alongside other young activists in numerous planning meetings and demonstrations for low-income housing, bilingual services, health care, workers' rights, fair treatment of immigrants, and affirmative action. They were among those who helped create the Danny Woo International District Community Garden, shoveling dirt and moving in railroad ties so that residents would have a place to till the soil and grow their own food. As their political awareness deepened, Silme and Gene began to speak out against the political repression of the Marcos dictatorship, a path that ultimately took them to their deaths.

But their contribution to the domestic labor movement on behalf of Asian American workers in the Alaska salmon-canning industry remains their most enduring legacy and is the subject of this retrospective publication. This story is told through the memories and reflections of the fellow activists who shared part of their life journeys with Silme and Gene. These activists were, in many cases, just as dedicated and committed as the two young men whose time is now history.

It is important to remember that Silme and

Silme Domingo at the University of Washington Asian Student Coalition dinner, fall 1973. *Courtesy* Asian Family Affair.

Gene were part of a much longer history of Asian workers on whose backs the lucrative commercial canning of salmon was built. Silme and Gene were not the first union leaders to speak out in the face of great peril or to come under surveillance, threat, and attack for their outspoken advocacy of workers' rights. They were not even the first to be killed. Silme and Gene knew they were stepping into danger, but their youthful passion for the cause—and their fearlessness—drove them headlong into a place they felt they needed to go in order to accomplish their goals. Backing off was not an option either would have considered.

Within days of the murders, the union reformers who worked with Silme and Gene at the ILWU set aside their personal fears and grief and returned to the blood-stained union hall, where they dispatched union members to jobs in Alaska under a new system free of the bribery and corruption that Silme and Gene had pledged to eliminate. As newly elected union officers, Silme and Gene didn't live to see their reforms come to pass, but union reformers stood fast in their commitment to seeing these changes institutionalized.

ILWU Local 37 still survives as Region 37 of the Inlandboatmen's Union. The union is currently housed in a modest office warehouse at Fishermen's Terminal in the Interbay neighborhood of Seattle. Three longtime activists—Silme's widow, Terri Mast, Rich Gurtiza, and John Foz—continue the robust advocacy for workers' rights that is both the immediate legacy of the Civil Rights Era of the 1960s and 1970s, which Gene and Silme represented, as well as the larger legacy of a militant Filipino-led union built on the dream of workers' rights, democracy, and solidarity with laborers around the globe.

Inspired by the knowledge of the union's proud yet turbulent history and guided by the continuing inspiration of Gene's and Silme's work, Region 37 leaders continue to fight the good fight. The task of organizing and representing workers in a rapidly changing seafood industry—during a time when union membership is on the decline and hostility toward immigrants is on the rise—is not easy. But it has never been easy. As Chris Mensalvas, Sr., president of Local 37, the inspirational hero to whom Gene and Silme both looked, wrote in 1952: "We will continue to fight as cannery workers, and fight we will until such time that our people can shout with the human courage and dignity of real workers!"

Industrial-Strength Life Lessons

In the 1960s and 1970s, the children of the first wave of Filipino American cannery workers grew into adolescence and began to follow their fathers to Alaska to take jobs in the canneries.

Alaska represented a distant place that connected them to the lives of their fathers. Members of the American-born generation hoped to earn money for the summer and return home in September after a demanding season of work. Most of them were also college-bound. In many families, they were the first generation to enter this place of privilege. For Gene and Silme and others of their generation, higher education provided a sheltered milieu for analyzing the world and seeing the Alaska experience in the context of Asian American history and the lingering presence of racial prejudice and discrimination against their people.

The young Alaskeros were incensed by what they saw and experienced in the canneries. They found the work tedious and grueling. The long hours took their toll, leading to exhaustion at the end of the day. The young cannery workers expressed amazement at the skill of some of the *manongs*, or "respected elders," men in their sixties and seventies who endured the strenuous pace for years on end, especially those who performed their tasks in the cold, wet fish house.

Andy Pascua, Gene Viernes's boyhood friend from Wapato, said that by the time he

Cannery in Egegik, Alaska.
IBU, Region 37 collection.

Gene Viernes took photos to document current working conditions in the canneries.
IBU, Region 37 collection.

and Viernes started going up to Alaska, most of the cannery crews still had at least several old men who were barely capable of working in the demanding jobs but needed the income to survive the winter. They passed the eye exams with help from others who spoke to them in Ilocano, directing them how to respond, and with urine samples provided by some of the younger Filipinos.

At the peak of the canning season, workers at the canneries put in eighteen-hour workdays. This created an increased hazard for the exhausted workers who operated the "Iron Chink," an automatic fish butchering machine derisively named for the skilled Chinese butchers it replaced. In 1978, Domingo confided in a letter, "I cut my hand in five places last night while cleaning the 'Iron Chink' (the first time I've been hurt in Alaska!) It's not bad, but it's pretty sore. It is a good thing I didn't get hurt more serious. I really need to struggle to be more conscious."

Bruce Occena, who worked one season at Uganik with Domingo in the late 1970s, said the butchers struggled to stay alert. "They'd just be literally dozing off and their hands were just

very close to these spinning saws," he recalled. As a slimer, working down the line from the butchers, part of Occena's job was to "keep an eye on the butchers." If the slimers saw any of the butchers starting to nod off, they would bang their knives to wake them up.

Pascua described working with his father in the fish house. On one occasion, the butchering machine malfunctioned. He told his father to shut off the machine. "You can't hear anything," he recalled. "It's loud. It's clanging, steaming, and all that. I reached in to get that salmon head, and I freaked. I pulled my arm out as fast as I could, and it sliced the raincoat off my arm. The blade took the raincoat."

Stan Viernes, Gene's younger brother, was also a slimer for four seasons. It was difficult for him because he was taller than most Filipinos and had to hunch to perform his job. "And you're in water, cold water, your hands are freezing, and you're just cleaning the fish nonstop," he said. A twenty-hour workday was common. When he woke up in the morning, he would find his hand frozen in a clenched position from holding the broad-handled sliming knife the day before. "My dad would come and grab my fingers, and he'd rub them and get the stiffness out of them," he said. "We would get it to where they were loose and he would put the knife in my hand and say, 'Let's get back to work.'"

Emma Catague worked at the Diamond E Fisheries cannery in Egegik in 1977 but couldn't stand the odor in the fish house because she was pregnant. She was transferred to the position of patcher. "The patching table actually is when they put the salmon in the can," she said. But after just five minutes, she continued, "you're going crazy" and your eyes "are going crossed" because the cans were going by so quickly. Finally, she was transferred to the can shop, where she fed sheets of metal into a machine to make the round cans.

Chris Mensalvas, Jr.—who worked for thirty-four years in the canneries, first at Red Salmon and then at Ketchikan—said he's held a variety of positions, starting as a slimer, which is considered the "dirtiest, the worst kind of job," and working his way up to warehouse positions. "I was really good with the casing machine, so I ended up doing that for many

Workers sort salmon roe.
IBU, Region 37 collection.

years," he said. "And then eventually, I became the warehouse foreman, and I was teaching other people to do that."

Mensalvas said the work in the canneries became a way of life for him even though he didn't, in truth, enjoy it. "It's really hard, physi-

Conditions in the fish house were cold, wet, and dangerous.
Gene Viernes photo. IBU, Region 37 collection.

cal labor," he said. "It just beats the hell out of you. But when you're with a lot of good friends, you just make things happen. You have a good time at the same time." Besides the camaraderie, the young cannery workers also liked the pay—several thousand dollars for a full season of labor, a tidy sum to take back home after they completed their stint.

Many of the canneries were located in remote, isolated areas, and Mensalvas and other young cannery workers said they would marvel at the stunning beauty of the pristine landscape, water, forests, and wildlife such as bears and eagles.

But for many young Alaskeros, their time in Alaska turned out to be a bitter bargain. As minorities, they were forced to eat inferior food in segregated mess halls and live in segregated run-down bunkhouses. They found the higher-paying jobs closed to them. The Alaska experience roused in Silme Domingo, Gene Viernes, and others a burning passion to fight for change.

Silme Domingo was born in Killeen, Texas, on January 25, 1952, the third of five children. His father, Nemesio Sr., hailed from Ilocos Sur Province and arrived in the United States in 1929 as part of the first large wave of immigrants from the Philippines before World War II. When he arrived, Nemesio Sr. was very poor. He lived with three other men in a hotel room in the International District. "We only had two pairs of shoes for all of us, so two of us slept in the day and two at night so we could use the shoes," he recalled, laughing.

Nemesio Sr. went to Alaska to work. He was at the San Juan Fishing Company cannery in Uganik Bay from 1936 until 1942, when he enlisted in the U.S. Army and returned to the Philippines to fight against the Japanese occupation. There, he met his wife, Ade, and returned to the United States to raise a family. Because of Nemesio Sr.'s military career, Silme and his siblings moved to various parts of the United States and stayed in Germany for several years. They eventually settled in Seattle, where Silme graduated with honors from Ballard High School. He went on to attend the University of Washington and graduated cum laude in 1975 with a bachelor's degree in political science.

In 1971, Domingo became an active member of the recently founded Asian Student Coalition (ASC) at the University of Washington.

Silme Domingo, at top center, joined with other protesters to confront then-City Councilman Liem Tuai at the groundbreaking ceremonies for the Kingdome.
Courtesy Asian Family Affair.

Chris Mensalvas, Jr. illustration. Courtesy International Examiner.

Across the United States, the Asian American movement coalesced on college campuses and in Asian communities as an outgrowth of the Civil Rights Movement and in response to the war in Vietnam. Although San Francisco, Los Angeles, and New York were important centers for the movement, it took hold in Seattle as well. Mass communication and inexpensive air travel facilitated the rapid movement of ideas and people.

Nationally, the movement was a response to discrimination, negative media images, and the legacy of oppression faced by the Asian community. Activists sought to uncover the "hidden history" of Asian immigrants and their contributions to American society and helped found inclusive ethnic studies courses that countered the persistent perception and portrayal of Asians as permanent aliens. The movement, inspired largely by the African American Civil Rights Movement, also moved outward from campuses and focused on the immigrant communities that continued to be infused with new arrivals seeking their share of the American dream despite the larger society's refusal to fully accept them.

In 1971, Domingo and other ASC activists started the short-lived *Kapisanan* newspaper in which they promoted their views and vision for change. The newspaper morphed into the *Asian Family Affair*, which began publishing in February 1972. Domingo became editor in 1973. But in the spring of 1974, after he met

Filipino American activist Russel Valparaiso, a member of the Yellow Brotherhood in Los Angeles, he began to shift his focus toward political events in the Philippines. He also began spending more time in the International District, where activists had begun to organize and fight for the preservation of family-run businesses and housing for low-income seniors and immigrant families.

The catalyst for the first large-scale direct action protests in the International District was construction of the Kingdome in 1972. King County planned this multipurpose stadium as a new home for professional football, baseball, soccer, and even basketball. But the siting of the stadium on the western edge of the International District threatened the neighborhood with traffic congestion, pollution, and the potential displacement of historic and current family-owned stores, restaurants, and hotels. Angered by the danger to the In-

Nemesio Domingo, Sr. (left) and Felix Viernes.

ternational District, Domingo and other student activists participated in demonstrations against the stadium and in support of funding for low-income housing and bilingual social services for the Asian community.

Government decision-makers dismissed the activists as loud-mouthed radicals. But it was the students' bold advocacy that provided the necessary passion to back negotiations on behalf of the neighborhood by established leaders like Bob Santos, then director of the International District Improvement Association, and businesspeople like Tomio Moriguchi and Shigeko Uno, who were likewise determined to protect community interests.

Gene Viernes was born on August 16, 1951, into a large working-class family in Wapato, Washington. His father, Felix, was Filipino; his mother, Betty, was Irish. Felix came from the small town of Urdaneta in Pangasinan Province. He arrived in Vancouver and worked his way south into Central Washington. Both Nemesio Sr. and Felix were part of the first large wave of Filipino migrant laborers who came to the United States before World War II. Like many other Filipinos in the Yakima Valley, Felix worked seasonally in the Alaska canneries and returned home to grow and harvest vegetables. His other jobs included operating a fruit stand, picking strawberries in Puyallup, and working as the night watchman at the Ross Packing Company in Selah.

Viernes was only fifteen when he made his first trek up to Alaska in 1967 with his father to work at a cannery operated by Wards Cove Packing Company in Ketchikan. He recalled his father paid a fifty-dollar bribe so that he could be maneuvered through a cannery union line-up to go to Alaska. Viernes worked that season in the fish house as a slimer. During his spare time, he worked in the egg house, lidding and strapping boxes, driving the forklift, and cleaning up.

The first season brought Viernes moments of trepidation. Legally, he was too young to work in the canneries, so he lied about his age. Pascua, who also accompanied his father to work at Wards Cove, said Viernes was small for his age. During an inspection of the bunk-house, "Gene jumped into the cook's oven to hide," Pascua recalled. "He came out. He was a little scared. We didn't know the oven was airtight."

Pascua said that working in Alaska was a humbling experience for "Wapato boys" like Viernes and himself. Even though they were among their lifelong friends, it was not the same as being on the farms. "If you got hot, your auntie would call you in and say, 'Have a pop because that's too much,'" he said. "These were people we didn't know. They were disrespectful. They didn't know us, and it was usually by race. So you have some guy coming in and ordering our fathers and uncles around, calling them 'Boy.' We had never seen that kind of overt stuff before, not in Wapato."

Viernes graduated from Wapato High School in 1969. Fiercely competitive, he was a state wrestling champion in high school. He supported himself through high school and college by working the first part of the summer in Alaska and then returning to the orchards and fields of the Yakima Valley. After starting at Yakima Valley Community College, he attended Central Washington State College for three years, majoring in history and the recently established ethnic studies program.

Working in Alaska was a tradition for both the Domingo and Viernes families. In the Domingo family, both Silme's older brother, Nemesio Jr., and younger sister, Lynn, worked in the canneries. In the Viernes family, Gene's younger brothers, Stan and Steve, also worked as Alaskeros.

Viernes developed an insatiable curiosity about history, especially the salmon-canning industry. He gathered a vast personal collection of documents and books on Filipinos and labor, materials that he freely shared with historians and friends. In the late 1970s, he compiled his research into a seven-part series on the history of the Alaska canneries for the *International Examiner*. Shortly thereafter, he became a regular staff writer for the mostly volunteer-run publication.

Domingo and Viernes were in college during a turbulent time, when student activism was at its height. Opposition to the draft and

Yakima Valley Community College wrestling team. Gene Viernes is on the far left.
Steve Viernes collection.

International Examiner staff, 1978. Back row (from left) Melody Leo, Lorraine Sako, Michael Cervantes, Gary Iwamoto, Julia Laranang, Jeanette Aguilar, Debbie Murakami, Randy Okimoto, Georgene Kumasaka, Mark Mano, Gene Viernes, Tim Otani, Anne Mori. Front (from left) Karen Chinn, Julie King, Kathy Chinn, Sue Chin, Vicki Woo, Ron Chew, Jesse Reyes.
John Harada photo. Courtesy International Examiner.

(From left) Bob Sotelo, Gene Viernes, and Andy Pascua, Red Salmon cannery, Naknek, Alaska, July 21, 1970. *Steve Viernes collection.*

the Vietnam War spread beyond college campuses as student protests escalated against a political establishment that continued to support and intensify the war.

Across the country, young Asian American activists, including Domingo and Viernes, returned to find their roots in the Chinatowns, Nihonmachis, and Little Manilas that represented their families' historic stake in American society. Seattle's International District was among the communities where activists worked to create grassroots solutions to persistent problems faced by Asian immigrant seniors, many of them current and former Alaskeros. Activists saw that too many elders, constrained by more than a century of social, economic, and legal discrimination, faced a daily struggle for survival in rodent-infested hotel rooms, without heat, adequate food, or health care.

For some young Filipino cannery workers, addressing the disparities in the canneries was an important front in the fight for justice. However, as Pascua and Viernes's younger brother Steve explained, their fathers and other *manongs* urged them not to cause trouble, reminding them, "You guys are in college. You only have to do this for a year or two." Additionally, the union representative was from Wapato, and they would have to contend with speaking out against a member of their own tight-knit community. "It's such a small community that everybody knows everybody else's business," Steve Viernes observed.

In 1972, circumstances changed for Viernes. Earlier in the year, his father passed away, and he felt freer to take action. During the 1972 season at Red Salmon, Viernes and Pascua discovered that the warehouse was stocked with fruit, vegetables, and juice reserved for "skilled" workers and company representatives. All summer long, they had feared they might develop scurvy, given their diet of rice, meat, and salmon heads. They were surprised by what they found in the warehouse. "We never saw any of that, and so while the cook had his back turned and was getting the rice, we shoved cans of peaches in our pockets, and then he would make me put them back," Pascua said. "While I was putting them back, Gene was stealing a fruit cocktail, and we just kept doing it. We eventually got away with two cans of fruit cocktail. We went back to the bunkhouse, and people were like, 'Oh, my God! Where did you get that?' And then, within a few days, we had an impromptu food strike because we knew they had the food. They just wouldn't give it to us."

At one point, Viernes tried to eat in the whites-only mess. He and other Filipino workers asked the cooks and foreman for fruit, vegetables, and juice. When their request was denied, Viernes stayed in his room and refused to eat for two days. Soon half of the crew—the younger members—joined him in boycotting the mess hall. Viernes became the spokesperson for the other strikers and took their petition to the union representative.

In 1973 at Wards Cove, Viernes used a different resistance strategy. He and other young cannery workers ate twice as much as normal, forcing the cooks to prepare more food. Then, at the next meal, they would refuse to eat. "It was just about the only way you could fight back," Pascua explained. Thereafter, the crew received fruit and fresh vegetables.

About the same time that Viernes and the young "Wapato boys" started to rebel, a group of "Seattle boys" began agitating for change as well. In 1970, Silme Domingo, his older brother, Nemesio Jr., and Michael Woo, a Chinese American, were working in the New England Fish Company (NEFCO) cannery at Uganik Bay. Domingo worked as a slimer, his brother was a waiter in the mess hall, and Woo was an egg puller. The Domingo brothers, who had worked for NEFCO since 1969, realized the cannery hadn't changed much since their father first worked there decades before. They even found "Nemesio Domingo—1942"

Gene Viernes, elected union delegate (steward) in the Dillingham plant, leads a crew meeting, 1979. *Steve Viernes collection.*

scratched on the bunkhouse wall. The walls were unpainted, the floor slanted toward the water, and the doors and windows had huge gaps in them, making the room drafty and cold.

According to Nemesio Jr., the younger Asian American workers sectioned off the bunkhouse with cardboard partitions. "We were told to take them down because they were a fire hazard," he said. At one point, a group went over to the white mess hall to get sandwiches and desserts, items not provided to the Filipinos. They were rebuffed. Nemesio Jr. said that when the superintendent overheard the young Asian American workers complaining, he went to the Filipino foreman, who "laid into" them about being ungrateful. "I think we felt bad about being dressed down like that by our elders," he recalled.

Woo said he was appalled at the awful living conditions at the cannery. Even though he and the Domingo brothers worked in different areas of the cannery, "we bonded around some of the working conditions and just being able to speak out about some of the conditions," he said. "I didn't come from a well-to-do family, but I didn't have holes in my walls where I slept." He said he could see outside through the cracks.

"Even in my time, automated laundry machines were pretty common. But up there, we actually had to crank our underwear and the few clothes that we had through a machine and try to hang them up to dry." Conversely, Woo saw that white workers—mostly college-age students or friends and relatives of management—lived in new, spacious, dormitory-style

Whites enjoyed a variety of foods in their mess hall unavailable to nonwhite cannery workers.
Steve Viernes collection.

facilities with modern laundry equipment. "We saw right away that there were some differences, and we wanted to speak out about it," he said.

Organizing

Dick Farinas, an investigator at the Equal Employment Opportunity Commission (EEOC) in Seattle, was the first person to move the complaints of the young cannery workers into the legal arena. During the 1960s and 1970s, the Civil Rights Act of 1964 became an important tool in the fight against workplace discrimination. One key section of the act, Title VII, banned employment discrimination on the basis of race, sex, religion, color, and national origin. The EEOC was the federal agency that enforced Title VII.

Farinas joined the EEOC in 1969 as an investigator, the first Filipino American ever hired for that position. He helped establish the EEOC office in Seattle in 1970. When the agency tapped him to investigate discrimination in the Alaska canneries, he already knew about the conditions from firsthand experience, having worked at three different canneries in Alaska in the early 1950s while a student at the University of Washington.

Years later, after he was hired at the EEOC, complaints about the unfair treatment of Filipinos in the Alaska canneries resurfaced. Farinas was approached by a young Filipino American from Seattle, Kevin Ebat, who had worked in a NEFCO cannery during the summer of 1972. "He was vocal in terms of trying to get the Filipino housing conditions and working conditions at par with the Caucasian employees," Farinas said. "Everything was so different—like in the white bunkhouses, the white employees don't wash their clothes. They were served. The company hired people to take care of their clothing, wash them, except for folding them. And they had their own separate bedrooms—each one of them." In contrast, Farinas said, the Filipino bunkhouse had a "line-up" of beds, or the workers laid their beds on the floor and slept on the floor.

On the basis of Ebat's complaint, Farinas fashioned an EEOC commissioner's charge against a number of Alaska canneries, alleging racial discrimination.

In 1971, after returning to Seattle, Silme and Nemesio Jr. received letters from the New England Fish Company (NEFCO) stating that the company would no longer employ them. Angry about being blacklisted, they asked their well-respected father to intervene on their behalf. Union president Gene Navarro met with the company, but it refused to back down. "The cannery management just simply walked out and said, 'They're still not coming back to the canneries,'" said Nemesio Jr. "I was still really ticked off about this."

They filed written complaints with the EEOC after talking to Farinas. The charges, Farinas said, were piggybacked on Ebat's original complaint.

Disappointed with the weak response from the leadership of Local 37 to their unfair treat-ment, Silme, his brother, and about two dozen other Asian American and Native American cannery workers returning from Alaska filed a class action lawsuit against NEFCO, the largest salmon-canning company in North America. The suit was filed in the fall of 1973 under Title VII of the 1964 Civil Rights Act.

The following spring, two similar lawsuits were filed: one against NEFCO-Fidalgo in Ketchikan, and another against Wards Cove Packing Company, Columbia Wards Fisheries, and Bumble Bee Seafoods.

When Viernes returned home from the 1973 season, he received a letter from the union informing him he was terminated by Wards Cove. The letter stated he was not fit to be rehired. He realized that—like the two Domingo brothers and the other young cannery workers involved in the lawsuits—he had been blacklisted.

The young activists formed the Alaska Cannery Workers Association to direct the lawsuits. The group was patterned after the United Construction Workers Association, a largely African American organization established in 1970 by Tyree Scott to open the construction trades to nonwhites. The cannery workers association adopted its constitution on October 12, 1973. Nemesio Domingo, Jr. and two Japanese Americans, Lester Kuramoto and Clarke Kido, served as the founding officers, with Silme Domingo and Michael Woo as advisers. It received support from the United Construction Workers Association, the United Methodist Church, the Presbyterian Church, and the Catholic Church.

Woo, who worked for the construction workers association after spending two seasons in Uganik Bay, played a key role in the formation of the cannery workers association. He said that Tyree Scott and Michael J. Fox, an attorney who represented the United Construction Workers Association and the United Farm Workers, sought to challenge employment discrimination in some new arenas: "Tyree was saying, 'Let's look for something.' I said, 'Hey, man. I used to work in the cannery, and I know these guys who worked with

continued on page 20

Settlement of the Class Action Discrimination Lawsuits

In 1973 and 1974, the Alaska Cannery Workers Association (ACWA) filed three class action lawsuits against the major cannery companies in Alaska, charging discrimination under Title VII of the 1964 Civil Rights Act.

Nemesio Domingo, Jr., former director of the association, recalled that when he and the other plaintiffs first took legal action against the salmon canning companies, they thought they would be pursuing a single lawsuit. But because of legal maneuvering by the industry, the suit was split into three cases. Domingo then spent the next two years "living out of a suitcase," traveling around to raise money to support the lawsuits. Their strategy, Domingo said, was to win one case, then use money from that settlement to pursue the second case and then the third. That approach worked surprisingly well for the first two cases, he observed, but it took many years to achieve success.

The Alaska Cannery Workers Association

Recently, Asian and Native American workers have come together to combat the long history of discrimination in the Alaska salmon canneries.

Rami Arditi, the attorney who spent much of his legal career on the three cases, began working on the lawsuits in March 1974 and didn't finish until twenty-seven years later, when the last case was finally put to rest.

He said that the lawsuits were, in the "broadest terms," about segregation in jobs, housing, and messing. The "practices were pretty striking," Arditi recalled, with bunkhouses and mess halls largely segregated and nonwhites staying in facilities that were referred to directly as the "Filipino bunkhouse" or "Native bunkhouse." Arditi noted that the ACWA class action lawsuits were tried in two phases: liability and then damages.

The first case, *Domingo v. New England Fish Co.*, was filed on behalf of nonwhites at New England Fish Company (NEFCO) facilities in Uganik, Chatham, Egegik, Waterfall, and Pederson Point. In addition to the Domingo brothers, the other plaintiffs were Sam Cabansag, Jr., Joseph C. Ancheta, Thomas G. Carpenter, Nellie Kookesh, Audrey A. Merculief, Frank Paul, Mary Paul, Tony Evon, Sr., and Samuel Strauss. It was first decided in federal district court by Judge Gus Solomon in November 1976. ACWA won on the issue of liability with a prima facie case of discriminatory employment practices in job allocation and in housing. But Solomon followed this initial ruling with a disappointing damages settlement in November 1981. By then, Terri Mast, Silme Domingo's widow, had been substituted for him in the lawsuit.

The case was appealed by both sides, with NEFCO appealing the liability ruling and ACWA appealing the ruling on damages. The court of appeals sent the case back down to a different district judge. The second time around, ACWA won again on the issue of liability and then won a substantial damage judgment. In 1980, while the NEFCO case was entangled in the appeals process, the company filed for bankruptcy, ostensibly because of the collapse of the Japanese market.

The second case to go to trial, *Carpenter v. NEFCO-Fidalgo Packing Co.*, yielded a broad court finding of liability in favor of the cannery workers in 1981, but there was never a trial on damages. The company agreed to settle the case out of court in 1985, providing cash settlements to each of the ten named minority plaintiffs: Thomas G. Carpenter, Sam Cabansag, Michael Cervantes, Benjamin Noma, Benjamin Presas, Robert Orlando, Ronald Festijo, Rod Mamon, Joseph C. Ancheta, and Salvador Castro. Money was also set aside to cover individual claims of housing and job discrimination.

Nemesio Domingo, Jr.
Dean Wong photo. Courtesy International Examiner.

The third class action lawsuit, *Atonio v. Wards Cove Packing Co.*, didn't come to trial until 1982. This case, which took twenty-seven years to settle, became a landmark Supreme Court decision against civil rights. Frank Atonio, the first named plaintiff, is a Samoan American. Gene Viernes was also a key plaintiff. His sister, Barbara, executor of his estate, was substituted for him in the lawsuit after his death. It was first tried before federal court judge Justin Quakenbush in Central Washington, who ruled against the plaintiffs on the issue of liability. A three-judge panel in the court of appeals affirmed that decision, but the ruling was later reversed during a larger en banc panel in front of eleven judges who came out strongly in favor of the plaintiffs.

Wards Cove then took the case to the Supreme Court. In 1989, as political winds changed and the Supreme Court took a decidedly conservative turn with the appointment of a fifth conservative judge to the Rehnquist court, the high court ruled five to four against the minority plaintiffs.

The U.S. Congress, alarmed by this decision and the continuing erosion of civil rights under the Supreme Court, passed the Civil Rights Act of 1991, which, in theory, bolstered the legal position of the cannery workers. But the Congress made an exception for the Wards Cove case because of political pressure from influential Alaska senator Frank Murkowski. After numerous appeals—and the case going back and forth between the district court and the court of appeals—the plaintiffs finally lost the case, their fight for justice falling victim to the strong conservative political tide in the country.

Arditi, who is now retired, said that there was a hopeful political climate when the Alaska Cannery Workers Association first launched its cases challenging the discrimination. "In the beginning, I think we all had the feeling that we were swimming with the current," he said. "And then there was a point when the current changed direction. We were swimming against the current even though we were swimming in the same direction as before."

During the early years of the lawsuits, the young plaintiffs were unable to enlist the support of the union leadership. Local 37 president and business agent Gene Navarro, who had run the union with an iron fist for many years, took an open stand against the cannery workers association, arguing that the group "is only an attempt to divide the existing membership" and to become a "bargaining agent" or rival union. When Navarro passed away in 1975, Tony Baruso, the longtime Boeing employee named to replace him, likewise kept the association at arm's length, refusing to embrace the challenges to the cannery companies. In time, Baruso's resistance to the efforts of the reformers set the stage for tragedy and renewal.

continued from page 17

me, and they're pissed off and they would do something.'" Woo told Scott about the Domingo brothers and other young Asian American activists who also worked in Alaska.

The construction workers association allocated funds for Woo and Silme Domingo to return to Alaska on an "observation trip" in July 1973 so that they could document the conditions. Woo and Domingo visited the canneries on the pretext that they were business administration students from the University of Washington, working on a summer project. In fact, they were there to talk to workers, take photographs, and gather names and addresses.

Farinas joined Woo and Domingo at the Uganik Bay cannery, where he planned to help gather information for the EEOC complaints. "They were there two days before I got there," Farinas said. He noted that Tony Diaz, the foreman, was from the same town as Domingo's father. "They know the family," he said. "They are close. So they let them go innocently walking around and taking notes."

The fact-finding trip included investigation of conditions at four canneries: NEFCO-Fidalgo and Wards Cove Packing Company, both in Ketchikan; Excursion Inlet Packing Company, a rural cannery; and Uganik Bay. By the time they got to Wards Cove, Woo recalled, "we got found out." The superintendent and foreman called Woo and Domingo into their office and told them the University of Washington didn't know who they were. The men added, "We're not sure why you're here, but you better get your ass off of here." That night, Woo and Domingo slept on the dock, waiting for the next float plane. "I guess we were happy to get out of there alive," Woo said.

Farinas prepared his own EEOC investigative report and sent his evidence to Washington, D.C. He invited cannery industry representatives to Seattle to take the necessary action to resolve the dispute. From 1972 through 1978, Farinas "went all over Alaska" to monitor the progress of the canneries in changing conditions for their minority workers. "It's a slow pace," he said. "They say, 'It's too much expense. We have been improving.'

I say, 'It's not me. Your complaint you got with the government, not me.' 'Okay, okay! We'll do our best, okay?'" At Chatham Cannery, the owners decided to close their facility rather than make the necessary adjustments. "I stated everything I wanted improved," Farinas remembered. "The Indian bunkhouse does not have heaters. During the canning season there, it gets around forty, fifty degrees. It is cold. They closed it because it would be enormously expensive on their part to really make it on par with the white employees."

After their trip, Woo and Domingo drafted a report charging that the salmon-canning industry was built on a system that relied on nonwhites, recruited through ILWU Local 37, to handle and can the fish, and whites, recruited through other hiring channels, to work in "skilled" positions. Whites worked as machinists, "beach gang" workers unloading fish from ships, and managers in the canneries. Nonwhites, meanwhile, were restricted to the most grueling and lowest-paid positions—sorting, cleaning, cutting, and canning the salmon. In essence, the industry conflated race with skill in order to justify unequal treatment of whites and nonwhites. There was no avenue for nonwhites to hire into the "skilled" jobs.

At Wards Cove, Woo and Domingo met Viernes, who had worked there for the past six seasons. In a letter to Domingo and Woo, Viernes warned the two that the company had seen through their cover and had made several token changes, including adding floor strips for traction in a hazardous spot, repairing an overhead drive apparatus, and changing the frequency of issuing fresh linen.

In the same letter, Viernes told Domingo and Woo: "This does not mean discrimination has ceased. The time I confronted the office for my weekly linen, they objected, reminding me of our previous policy. I told them that it was a bunch of bull." He also described his struggle to get medical treatment for an "old buffalo," an older worker who had cut his head on an overhead belt in the fish house. "He went to the office & requested medical attention," Viernes's letter stated. "They told him to come back tomorrow. I, after hearing about this, got pissed and led him back to the office to bitch & get my linen." After an argument—and being told that the old man would not be able to see a doctor until the next day—Viernes was finally able to get some antiseptic and some bandages from the superintendent.

Viernes detailed a litany of other concerns as well, including a can-catching apparatus that was constantly breaking. "Twice in two days, the thing has fallen apart & injured workers' feet," he wrote. "We yelled at the mechanics & they stopped the line." The workers then requested "proper footwear" and were told that "for the last 50 yrs. no one ever wears special footwear & that it wasn't necessary."

Viernes described the unequal provision of juice to the Filipino crew compared with the white crew and "miscellaneous work" the Filipino crew was forced to do "outside of contract time & compensation." "We have been required to climb on the side of hills, carrying bolo knives to cut down grass for the beautification of the cannery. Thankfully no one was hurt, though many slipped several times."

A meticulous observer, Viernes detailed what he observed and listed the witnesses to each occurrence. He took snapshots and kept careful notes, creating a trail of evidence for the lawsuits. David Della, another young cannery worker from Seattle, drove to Central Washington with Silme Domingo in the mid-1970s to meet Viernes for the first time. They found him living in a trailer just outside of Wapato. After spending several days with him, they learned that he was documenting the early history of the Filipino community in Wapato. They encouraged him to come to Seattle and get to know other activists there.

As the organizing efforts of the Alaska Cannery Workers Association intensified, Woo and ACWA director Sam Cabansag went on a two-and-a-half week trip to California

A portion of a letter from Gene Viernes to Michael Woo and Silme Domingo in 1973, describing intolerable cannery conditions.
Ron Chew collection.

just before the 1974 salmon-canning season, planning to make contact with migrant field workers who worked in Alaska during canning season. This trip was also funded by the United Construction Workers Association. They visited San Francisco, Oakland, Delano, Earlimart, Stockton, and San Jose and met with young cannery activists as well as *manongs* who had worked in the industry for years. They were looking for potential plaintiffs.

In San Francisco, Woo reconnected with Jerry Abasolo, whom he first met at Wards Cove during the observation study trip to Alaska. Abasolo told Woo and Cabansag that the crew, which consisted of sixty-five members of Local 37, had participated in a "wildcat strike" and had "submitted a petition of their grievances to the management" signed by fifty workers and the older Filipino foreman.

In Stockton, home to a huge population of Filipino Americans, many residents recognized the Cabansag name and showed great

We can have the final word on equal opportunity.

Join us in protests against the Supreme Court ruling against affirmative action in the Bakke case.

- **Saturday, July 1:** Picket at federal courthouse in Seattle, 5th Ave. and Madison, 10:30 a.m.
- **Saturday, July 8:** Picket at federal courthouse, 10:30 a.m.
- **Saturday, July 15:** Civil rights march in Seattle. (Watch for details.)

The National Committee to Overturn the Bakke Decision shared the ACWA office.
Ron Chew collection.

interest in learning about the ACWA effort. Woo and Cabansag discovered that most of the older men had been agricultural laborers but preferred work in the canneries because it was not as physically demanding. As a result, they hesitated to join the fight against the discriminatory policies of the canneries, which were their only source of income. According to Woo and Cabansag's report: "Older men would say, 'Oh, I wish I were younger . . . I would like to help you.' We told them 'not to help us, but to help us *all*.' But they could only offer their moral support."

At the close of their stay in Delano, Woo and Cabansag visited Agbayani Village just outside of town. United Farm Workers (UFW) union volunteers had built the sixty-unit retire-

ment village in 1973 for aging Filipino laborers who had worked the fields of California; many retirees were bachelors because of California's racist anti-miscegenation laws, which were repealed only in 1962. There, Woo and Cabansag spoke to Philip Vera Cruz, longtime vice president of the UFW. Vera Cruz, an agricultural worker and labor organizer, helped spearhead the dramatic 1965 grape strike in the fields of Delano, which led to the formation of the union and the rise of Cesar Chavez as its leader.

Back in Seattle, the Alaska Cannery Workers Association established an office at 416 Eighth Avenue in the International District, separate from the ILWU Local 37 union hall. Robert Chinn, founder of the United Savings and Loan Bank, told Woo about the space across from the Four Seas Restaurant. "I don't remember who the property owner was, but the Hip Sing Tong—my father was president of the Hip Sing for a long time—my father knew this guy. So when I said, 'I'm Frank Woo's son,' he said, 'Oh, yeah. I'll lease it.'"

At the time, it was unusual for a small nonprofit organization to have an office. The ACWA headquarters quickly became an all-purpose gathering place where young Asian American activists were able to strategize, develop community support, and meet with potential class members, especially older Filipino cannery workers who lived in nearby hotels and continued to work in the industry. The ACWA office quickly became the regular meeting space, mail drop, and message center for a host of groups including Women in Trades, Committee for Corrective Action, National Committee to Overturn the Bakke Decision, and International District Farmers Market. The Wing Luke Museum, the first pan-Asian Pacific American community museum in the country, was located next door to the ACWA office, so the street became a colorful and well-trafficked corner of the International District.

Sam Cabansag served as the first ACWA director and was followed shortly thereafter by Nemesio Domingo, Jr. Meanwhile, Silme Domingo recruited Julia Laranang, a local Filipina whose father had worked in Alaska, to serve as the office manager after meeting her at a protest against martial law in the Philippines at the University of Washington. A young white woman, Terri Mast, who had worked as a cook in an Alaska cannery, joined the staff as well, helping with research for the class action lawsuits and outreach to potential class members. "The staff was actually paid through what's now called the AmeriCorps, but it was the local VISTA [Volunteers in Service to America]," Laranang said. "We were all VISTA volunteers."

Apart from its legal work, the cannery workers association began publishing the *International Examiner*, a free newspaper first established in 1974 by two young businessmen in the International District. The paper provided a community voice for the small businesses, young professionals, arts organizations, and bilingual social service agencies that sprang up in the late 1960s and early 1970s.

The cannery workers association acquired the newspaper in 1977 after ACWA director Nemesio Domingo, Jr. purchased it for one dollar and published it until 1980, when it incorporated as an independent nonprofit organization. Although the newspaper's content took on a stronger social justice tone when the association became publisher, it was under no pressure to do so. The newspaper staff believed in advocacy journalism. Many were the first in their families to attend college and pursue journalism as a career. Some had established a coalition at the University of Washington, called Third World People in Communications, and published the *Northwest Access* newspaper in 1976 and 1977. Nemesio Jr. took a hands-off role as publisher of the *International Examiner*, allowing the content to be determined by an independent editor and staff.

The *Examiner* served as a training ground for a generation of writers, photographers, and artists. Viernes not only contributed a seven-part series on the history of the Alaska canneries, he also wrote other articles on the ACWA lawsuits and the future of the salmon-canning industry. Other young cannery-worker activists—including Silme Domingo and Alonzo Suson—wrote news articles about Filipino community events and the anti-Marcos move-

International Examiner
"The Heartbeat of the International District"

November 1975

Francisca Abuel (left) and Estelita Almirante (right) complain that working conditions in the Philippine counsel's home were intolerable.
photo by Elaine Ko

Filipinas Faced with Deportation

Two Filipina maids who fled what they call bad working conditions under the Philippine Consul General are now faced with deportation for violating their diplomatic status.
The International Drop-In Center has taken up the defense of the two women, Francisca Abuel and Estelita

"They," Guerzon said, "are not complaining so much about salary as they are the fact that they were used in the business of daycare."
The women, Guerzon charged, worked as attendants in the nursery of Palarca without being paid normal wages for that type of work. "It's in

"I believe that the public disclosure of our treatment and working conditions has caused great embarrassment to the government of the Philippines.
"I fear that if I return to the Philippines, the government will persecute me because I have exposed its treatment of its own citizens. I have

REVIEW BOARD ELECTIONS FORTHCOMING

Elections are forthcoming for the International District Special Review Board. On Tuesday, November 18, three positions will be filled on the Board.
The Board was established to promote and preserve the cultural, economic and historic qualities of the ID. The Board came about in answer to the need for special solutions to the District's complex problems. It is comprised of a cross-section of community interests.
Candidates for the positions are as follows:

Position 3: Tomio Moriguchi

Position 4: Alexander Bishop
Faye Hong

Position 5: Jack Buttnick
Tommy Quan
Allen Claiborne

Polling places for the November 18 elections are at International Terrace, 206 6th Ave. S.; Inter*im, 627 S. Jackson; Wing Luke Museum, 414 8th Ave. S.; and Chong Wah Hall, 522 7th Ave. South.

ment in the U.S., either anonymously or under pseudonyms. Chris Mensalvas, Jr., John Foz, and David Della contributed illustrations.

The newspaper was housed at the ACWA office until April 1979, when it moved to the Jackson Building. By then, ACWA organizers had launched a full-bore union reform effort and wanted the newspaper to stand on its own and have the independence to investigate whatever it chose, rather than be tethered to the specific activities and interests of the cannery workers association.

Rediscovering the History of ILWU Local 37

By the time young college-educated Asian Americans began working in Alaska, the leadership of the union had become part of the problem. Despite improvements won in the early years of the union, working conditions in the canneries remained hazardous and cannery owners still restricted nonwhite workers to low-paying jobs and substandard segregated housing. Nonwhite workers were forced to perform menial tasks outside the scope of their contracts. They wondered why their union leaders did not demand changes. When had they lost their union?

Silme Domingo and Gene Viernes began researching the history of the union and rediscovered the stories of militant trade unionists from the 1930s and 1940s, many of whom still had close ties to the union but were no longer in positions of power. The two young activists brought different talents to this endeavor. With his talkative nature and Seattle roots, Domingo was able to make personal connections to old-timers in Seattle who could share stories of the past. Viernes's natural love of historical research and his roots in Wapato helped him piece together a paper trail into the past and draw forth additional voices from Central Washington.

They learned that Local 37 was born out of the concerted efforts of Virgil Duyungan and other labor pioneers who began organizing in

Harry Bridges, ILWU President.
1952 ILWU Yearbook. *IBU, Region 37 collection.*

fields and canneries as early as the 1920s. Their efforts bore fruit when they established the Cannery Workers and Farm Laborers Union (CWFLU) in 1933.

Before 1933, cannery workers were subject to a repressive contract labor system in which they were treated much like indentured servants. They had no collective bargaining rights and few protections against poor treatment and workplace hazards.

After getting rid of the contract labor system, the union began to evolve as a voice for Filipino immigrant laborers, who frequently found themselves at the bottom of the economic and political ladder. Since its formation, the union had struggled with various government attempts to deport militant union leaders, internal scandals, and an industry driven by an unending desire to maximize profits. These challenges resulted in a succession of leadership battles and the formation of competing labor groups split along ethnic lines.

By 1937, the CWFLU established ties with militant leftist longshoremen, and the membership voted overwhelmingly to reaffiliate with the Congress of Industrial Organizations (CIO), becoming Local 7 of the United Cannery, Agricultural and Packinghouse and Allied Workers of America.

In the late 1940s, several Local 7 factions fought bitterly for control. By 1947, Local 7 had become part of the Food, Tobacco, Agricultural and Allied Workers' Union of America. Leaders of competing factions in Local 7 broke away and founded a competing organization, the Seafood Workers Union. After a 1950 vote, Local 7 won the right to represent cannery workers. It affiliated with the International Longshoremen's and Warehousemen's Union and became known as Local 7-C; in the fall of 1951, Local 7-C became Local 37.

Local 7's affiliation with the ILWU brought together two organizations well known for their militant approach toward securing workers' rights. The ILWU was founded in 1937 shortly after efforts to organize shore workers on the West Coast precipitated violent strikes. Under its first president, Harry Bridges, the ILWU expanded rapidly, representing dock workers and related workers throughout the West Coast and Hawaii.

During the rabid anti-Communist era of the 1950s, the ILWU International's leadership, as well as Local 37 officers, were harassed, jailed, and threatened with deportation. In response, the union fell into a period of entrenched passivity and conservatism, despite the best efforts of its remaining progressive voices. This is the organization that Viernes and Domingo inherited when they began their reform efforts in the 1970s. Despite the years of corruption and mismanagement, they hoped to return the union to its earlier militant roots, when it had been an organization that drew its strength from democratic representation, strong rank-and-file participation, and direct action in pursuit of workers' rights.

Viernes and Domingo were emboldened when they learned that ILWU Local 37 had a proud tradition of rank-and-file democracy

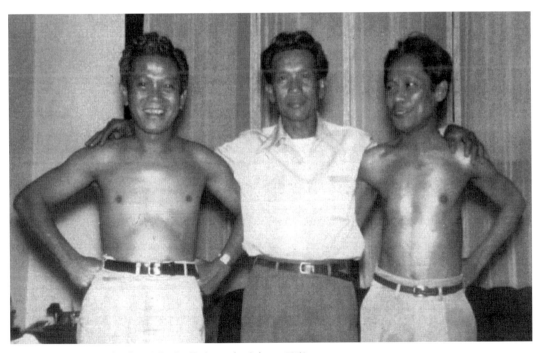

Chris Mensalvas, Sr. (left) and Carlos Bulosan (right), ca. 1950s.
Chris Mensalvas, Jr. collection.

based on the active engagement of members who pushed for change from the bottom up. They found inspiration in the wider history of the ILWU International's tradition of labor radicalism and militant resistance forged under Bridges's leadership. Basing their plans for change on the admirable struggle of the *manongs* who built the union from the 1930s to the 1950s, Viernes and Domingo prepared a road map for renewed reform efforts.

A personal mentor for the reformers was Chris Mensalvas, Sr., the real-life cannery union organizer who was the inspiration for one of the main characters in Carlos Bulosan's classic *America Is in the Heart*. A close friend of Bulosan's, Mensalvas was retired, living in a low-income apartment building in Seattle's International District. But his powerful organizing skills among farm and cannery workers remained legendary.

Mensalvas, a union pioneer and a member of the Communist Party, was harassed for many years by immigration authorities who tried unsuccessfully to deport him. He served as president of Local 37 from 1949 to 1959 at the height of the anti-Communist purges. In addition to his leadership of the Seattle-based cannery union, Mensalvas helped organize the first major strike of agricultural workers in Stockton after World War II. Viernes had a ready connection to the legendary organizer; he had worked with Mensalvas's son, Chris Mensalvas, Jr., at the Red Salmon cannery.

The young reformers realized that if they hoped to create change in the industry, they had to first take back the union and began working toward becoming leaders in the union. Moreover, they realized that the Alaska Cannery Workers Association lawsuits, as well-intentioned as they were, created a perception problem among elder Alaskeros who remembered when cannery companies supported dual unions to divide workers and undermine union organizing efforts. Even though ACWA members assured the elders that theirs was a legal advocacy group, not another competing union, many *manongs* remained skeptical of their motives.

In exploring the union's history, Viernes and Domingo also discovered the ILWU International's history of support for trade union rights around the world and opposition to repressive regimes overseas. In the 1930s, the ILWU blocked the

Filipino Americans organized protests in downtown Seattle to draw attention to abuses under Marcos. At left is Celia Rodriguez. *Sumi Hayashi photo. Courtesy* International Examiner.

Gene Viernes shares information about union reform efforts at an International District summer festival booth in front of the Kokusai Theater on Maynard Avenue, late 1970s.
Steve Viernes collection.

shipment of supplies to the rising fascist movements in Europe and Asia. After World War II, the union opposed escalation of the arms race and the Cold War. In the early 1960s, the ILWU opposed American military intervention in Vietnam.

Because ILWU Local 37 had a heavy concentration of Filipino American laborers, it consistently and forcefully opposed colonial control of the Philippines, repression of Philippine trade unionists in the early 1950s, and supported the Hukbalahap guerrilla movement. The union's leaders were vulnerable to charges of subversion, especially during the 1950s when four Local 37 leaders—Ernesto Mangaoang, Chris Mensalvas, Sr., Joe Prudencio, and Ponce Torres—were detained at length for their political beliefs and targeted for deportation.

The ACWA reformers realized that working for social and economic justice against the capitalist status quo was in keeping with the finest tradition of the ILWU and the vision of Local 37's earlier leaders. Domingo and Viernes, as committed leaders in the Seattle chapter of the Union of Democratic Filipinos (Katipunan ng mga Demokratikong Pilipino) or KDP, and the Anti-Martial Law Coalition, saw the fight within the union as part of a larger ongoing international battle against economic repression.

Founded in California in 1973, the Union of Democratic Filipinos was a U.S.-based movement with up to ten chapters throughout the country that sought to counter President Ferdinand Marcos's repression of democratic rights in the Philippines. In 1972, Marcos had declared martial law, prompting widespread opposition both in the Philippines and abroad. In 1974, Dale Borgeson, a Swedish American KDP leader from California, recruited Domingo and another Seattle activist, Angel Doniego, into the organization. Later that year, Domingo, Doniego, and others founded a Seattle chapter, which grew to become the largest and most ethnically diverse of the chapters, boasting more than forty members.

The Seattle chapter formed teams that addressed specific political and social concerns such as youth violence, poverty, social services for the elderly and immigrants, housing disparities, and development threats to the International District. It also joined the ongoing fight for better conditions for Filipino cannery workers. In 1975, Domingo recruited Viernes into the Union of Democratic Filipinos in an effort to bridge efforts between the Local 37 and the KDP. The infusion of KDP grassroots political activism into the cannery workers association's reform efforts caused ACWA members to refocus their energies on trying to change the ILWU from within.

Meanwhile, Domingo's work with the Union of Democratic Filipinos continued to expand outward into the community. He began to get more involved with the Filipino Community of Seattle (FCC) and helped found Filipinos for Action and Reform (FAR), which fought for immigrant rights and supported efforts to educate the public about repression in the Philippines. In 1978, he and several other members of Filipinos for Action and Reform were elected to the Filipino Community of Seattle. However, in 1980, following a bitterly fought contest, a number of FAR candidates lost in the election.

Domingo also played a leading role in initiating the Philippine National Day celebration in Seattle, held to commemorate the declaration of Philippine independence in 1898. The barrio fiesta event emphasized pride in cultural achievements and cultural roots.

The Rank-and-File Committee

After being blacklisted, Domingo and Viernes pursued legal action to force the union and the companies to rehire them to work in Alaska. They realized that they needed to go back to Alaska so that they were not just plaintiffs in

class action lawsuits, but activists engaged directly with the workers from within the industry. After arguing successfully that they were victims of retaliation for complaining about conditions at the canneries, Silme Domingo returned to work at the New England Fish Company's Uganik Bay cannery and Gene Viernes was dispatched to the Peter Pan Seafoods Dillingham cannery.

In 1977, the union reformers created the Rank-and-File Committee, modeled after earlier reform movement efforts in Local 37 led by Chris Mensalvas, Sr. "There was no way in which we were going to sustain our efforts in the lawsuits without having the union aboard," David Della recalled. "We came up with our plan on what we were going to do, starting with fair dispatch, bring back organizing, strengthen the shop steward system, and, at some point, the finances of the union." The reformers also decided to take up safety issues. At that time, the canneries used very old, unsafe machinery, some of which dated to the early 1900s. Without adequate safeguards, people sometimes lost their fingers or hands.

They spread their message among workers by printing and distributing the "Rank-and-File" newsletter, which urged implementation of a "progressive program that spoke to workers' problems." The Rank-and-File Committee realized that communication was vital to a successful reform movement among a seasonal migratory labor force. Many workers lived and worked in Central Washington or California and traveled to Alaska only in the summer to work in the canneries.

Committee members produced the newsletter in the back room of the ACWA office on a low-quality offset printing press. Viernes not only wrote many of the articles in the newsletter; he also operated the press. The newsletter harked back to 1946, when, as it explained, "workers were disgusted with conditions in the canneries and the lack of action by union officials on their just complaints." At that time, Chris Mensalvas, Sr., Leo Lorenzo, and others established a Rank-and-File Committee.

In one newsletter, distributed several months after the Rank-and-File Committee

List of All
DISPATCH DATES

List of All
FIRST PREFERENCE CREW

DO NOT REMOVE

(From left) Juan Crisostomo, Alonzo Suson, John Foz, Brian Hixson, Angel Doniego, and Lynn Domingo in the union hall. The dispatch bulletin board was one of the first improvements of the reform movement. *John Stamets photo.*

was established, Domingo and Viernes, chairman and secretary, respectively, complained that Local 37 had "lost much of its former strength and militancy," pointing to the drop from fifty contracts to twenty and the decline in membership from more than four thousand to less than nine hundred. Asking for contributions of "$2 or $5 or more," the newsletter stated that the Rank-and-File Committee was committed to fighting for union democracy and honesty in union affairs.

The newsletter hammered on the importance of creating a fair dispatch system. By the 1960s and 1970s, corruption and payoffs were endemic among union officials. Often, workers got to go to Alaska because they knew the dispatcher or one of the foremen and were willing to bribe their way into a job. Dispatchers also gave preference to those involved in the lucrative gambling operations in the canneries instead of following the three-tier preference system delineated in the union contract.

Official union rules specified anyone who had worked in a cannery the previous year had the first preference for being hired the next year. A person who had worked for that company, but at a different plant, had the second preference to be hired by that company. And anyone who had worked anywhere in the industry the year before had third preference to be hired if there was an opening.

"You will find people at the end of the dispatch season who didn't pay a bribe, didn't know a foreman, didn't have a connection, and

Sample Ballot

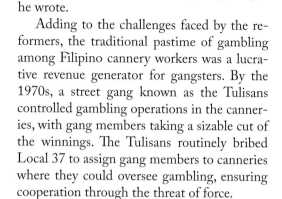

PRESIDENT/BUSINESS AGENT (VOTE FOR ONE):
[ ] Tony Baruso
[ ] Peter Bautista

VICE-PRESIDENT (VOTE FOR ONE):
[✔] Nemesio Domingo Sr.
[ ] King Monillas

SECRETARY/TREASURER (VOTE FOR ONE):
[ ] Ponce Torres
[ ] Rudy (Amin) Abella
[✔] Gene Viernes

DISPATCHER (VOTE FOR ONE):
[ ] Rudy "Tambok" Nazario
[ ] Ted Daddeo
[✔] Silme Domingo

PATROLMAN (VOTE FOR ONE):
[✔] Pantal Cabuena

TRUSTEES (VOTE FOR THREE):
[ ] Salvador Del Fierro
[ ] Alex Arnejo
[ ] Gene Domingo
[ ] Marian Bautista
[✔] John Hatten
[ ] Santiago Tordilles

EXECUTIVE BOARD (VOTE FOR NINE):
[ ] Benny Caluya
[✔] Henry Ceridon
[ ] Max Salvador
[✔] Chris Mensalvas Jr.
[ ] Albert Cruz
[✔] Sam Cabansag Jr.
[✔] Ricardo Farinas Jr.
[✔] Emma Catague
[✔] Sue Williams
[✔] Nick Facelo

Rank-and-File Committee candidates, 1978.
Ron Chew collection.

Sue Williams
IBU, Region 37 collection.

'compadre' or 'kabayaan,' but a system that can fairly choose for dispatch from a pool of workers that outnumber the available job openings," he wrote.

Adding to the challenges faced by the reformers, the traditional pastime of gambling among Filipino cannery workers was a lucrative revenue generator for gangsters. By the 1970s, a street gang known as the Tulisans controlled gambling operations in the canneries, with gang members taking a sizable cut of the winnings. The Tulisans routinely bribed Local 37 to assign gang members to canneries where they could oversee gambling, ensuring cooperation through the threat of force.

As the young organizers headed to Alaska again, they began working closely together, learning how to be effective organizers by trial and error, critically analyzing their work along the way. Soon, the Rank-and-File Committee movement began to grow. Committee members found their way into every cannery. They were elected as shop stewards and began to aggressively take up workers' issues on the shop floor, gaining respect and greater support from the other union members.

The reformers wrote to each other regularly, describing their ongoing challenges. In a 1978 letter to Viernes, Domingo described his efforts at Uganik to prepare fellow workers for a visit by federal inspectors. Domingo saw the cannery owners rushing to implement upgrades to the facilities, but doubted they were serious about making permanent changes. "It was really evident that NEFCO was really trying to showcase this entire situation," he wrote. "For example, for the first time in ten years, the toilets finally flushed!"

To rally workers to the reform cause, Domingo organized visits to the white bunkhouses, traditionally off limits to Filipinos and other nonwhite workers. "We even set up tours

they're continuing to come to the hall, and it's just the last few bodies at the end of the season," John Foz explained. "There's only one or two more dispatches left, and there's a handful of people that are still trying to get up and who, of course, would never get up under the old system."

The favoritism that determined who was dispatched—the "compadre system"—was targeted for elimination by the young reformers. Viernes, running for the position of dispatcher on the Rank-and-File Committee slate, called for strict adherence to the contract. "What our union needs is not an arbitrary system with the of the 'Uganik Hilton' (new machinist bunkhouse) prior to people's interviews. These did wonders agitating peoples' sense of injustice," Domingo wrote.

The Rank-and-File Committee's successes allowed them to feel confident enough to field candidates for the 1978 election, when they won several positions on the executive board. Emma Catague and Sue Williams were the first women ever elected to serve on that board. However, Viernes lost his bid to become secretary-treasurer, and Domingo did not win the race for dispatcher.

In 1980, when the secretary-treasurer of Local 37 died, Domingo was appointed to finish out the term. Later that year, Rank-and-File Committee members took every position in Local 37 except the presidency. Because they did not vie for the top post, incumbent Tony Baruso easily won reelection. Terri Mast, then a Rank-and-File Committee member, believes the decision to not challenge Baruso was a mistake because the reformers probably had a better chance of ousting him than they thought. In that year's election, Domingo was elected secretary-treasurer and Viernes became dispatcher. Mast was elected to the executive board. They had only just begun to implement

their reform program when Silme Domingo and Gene Viernes were gunned down in the union hall after the very first fair dispatch of the season.

Dangerous Waters

As their work with the Union of Democratic Filipinos expanded the scope of their political work, Domingo and Viernes intensified their activism against Marcos, reaching out to fellow labor activists in the Philippines. But the issue of Marcos and martial law in the Philippines created a deep and contentious split in the community. Many of the older generation, who were from the Ilocos region where Marcos was born, felt a sense of kinship with the Philippine leader even though they might have been ambivalent about his repressive politics. Many of the younger activists and recent immigrants who had experienced human rights violations under Marcos were outspoken in their opposition to Marcos, offending many elders. The fierce split between the two sides sometimes erupted at Filipino Community Center meetings and at the Filipino People's Far West Conventions. "There were some seri-

Cannery industry representatives meet with ILWU Local 37 officers to negotiate union contracts. Local 37 representatives include Salvador del Fierro, Sr. (far left), Pete Bautista (second from left), Silme Domingo (third from left), Tony Baruso (seated at center), and Ponce Torres (on Baruso's left).
Ron Chew collection.

ous, serious, public, almost knock-down, drag-out fights," Laranang recalled.

Within the ILWU International, awareness of the split over support for Marcos led to an unprecedented silence. Despite the ILWU leadership's long tradition of opposition to repressive regimes around the world, the union avoided the issue in order to maintain stability within the large block of Filipino American ILWU members.

KDP reformers within Local 37 remained outspoken. In his attempts to persuade others, Domingo would share a simple story about what had happened when his grandmother and a friend of hers went to vote in a supposedly free election. His grandmother's friend voted against Marcos using a "secret ballot." When her friend returned home after voting, the police told him, "You better go back and vote right if you know what's good for you."

By 1981, the reformers were increasingly aware of the multiple forces aligning against them. In early March, recently ousted Local 37 dispatcher Rudy Nazario was gunned down in the parking lot outside his apartment in South Seattle. Many suspected the Tulisan gang, headed by Fortunato "Tony" Dictado.

In April 1981, Viernes made a trip to the Philippines to meet with anti-Marcos opposition leaders, including members of the May First Movement (Kilusang Mayo Uno), or KMU, a federation of anti-Marcos trade unions with a combined membership of 500,000. He and May First Movement leaders planned for the organization to host a delegation from the ILWU that would investigate the conditions of Filipino workers. Afterwards, Viernes travelled directly to the ILWU International Convention in Honolulu where he and Domingo

Gene Viernes speaking at the ILWU convention in Honolulu, 1981.
Emily Van Bronkhorst collection.

led a vigorous fight to pass a resolution to send an investigating team to the Philippines. The issue put the divisions over the Marcos regime on full public display. ILWU Local 142 Hawaii, legendary for its cohesive voting, split for the first time in memory. The resolution passed after an impassioned speech by Viernes, despite the opposition of Baruso and other Marcos supporters within the ILWU.

"This action was a direct threat to the Marcos dictatorship because the labor movement was the one area where he had little support because of his brutal attacks on labor and because of the no-strike decree that he had created that was part of his regime," Terri Mast later explained. "The support of the ILWU for the KMU, the largest trade union federation in the Philippines, had just been sealed. And any disruptions of cargo into or out of the Philippines would have a major economic impact on the country."

In the years since the murders, allies of Viernes and Domingo have pointed to the Hawaii convention as the precipitating event that led to their deaths. Many who knew the two now recall the ominous signs. At the Hawaii ILWU convention, Viernes asked Domingo's sister, Cindy, to buy the Polaroid snapshot taken as he delivered his address at the podium. When Cindy refused, Viernes offered to pay for it, explaining, "I don't want the agents to have that picture."

After the ILWU convention, Lynn Domingo recalled, "Silme actually came to me and the executive board and said, 'We need to buy life insurance.'" Meanwhile, she noticed that when she was driving his car, another vehicle would follow her. "I told Silme, 'Somebody's following you.' He started laughing. Nobody believed me, right? And I was like, 'No, there *is* someone following you, Silme. This is your car.'" This occurrence, coupled with a telephone conversation with her sister, Cindy, during which the "phone started to act real weird," heightened the sense of anxiety she felt in the week before the murders.

Steve Viernes remembered that after his brother returned from the Philippines, the two spent a week together before Steve went to Alaska to help with early preparations at the cannery where he was working. Out of the blue, Gene told Steve that he had been followed as he was driving Steve's truck. He warned Steve to be careful. "I was like, 'Are you kidding me?'" Steve recalled. "He just said that he noticed there were people in the background."

Angel Doniego, the individual who recruited Domingo to join the Union of Democratic Filipinos in the early 1970s, said he had warned Domingo early on to be careful around the union hall. On one occasion, Doniego and Domingo discussed the 1936 murders of Virgil Duyungan and Aurelio Simon, two cannery union leaders who had fought to eliminate the cannery contractor system and were shot to death at the Gyokko Ken restaurant in Seattle's Chinatown. "I used to tell Silme, 'You need to start carrying a weapon in that desk of yours.' He would say, 'Ah, don't worry about this shit. Yeah, I got it covered.' I used to say, 'Yeah, right.

Maybe one of these days, man, you know?'"

Doniego, a vocal opponent of the Marcos regime, had his own reasons to be vigilant. In the early morning on June 7, 1977, he was stopped and harassed by four men claiming to be plainclothes Seattle police officers. They ordered him to provide a list of Filipino community activists and stop his political activities. If he didn't, Doniego recalled them saying, he would be "put away" and his family would face repercussions. At one point during an hourlong interrogation, one of the men punched him, and he was left lying on the ground.

While Domingo traveled to Alaska in the spring of 1981, Terri Mast filled in for him at the ILWU Local 37 hall. In the days before June 1, Mast saw Tulisan gang member Jimmy Ramil enter the hall and meet with Tony Baruso in his office. The door remained closed for almost an hour. Nazario's recent death at the hands of gangsters made all of them aware of their vulnerability. Mast remembered feeling that this was a sign that the forces aligned against the reformers were escalating to a very dangerous level.

June 1, 1981

On June 1, 1981, tensions were high at the union hall in anticipation of the first Alaska dispatch under the reform leadership. Viernes, newly installed as dispatcher, was determined to keep his pledge to eliminate bribery and favoritism, angering those who counted on the old system that sent them to Alaska, where they could run lucrative gambling operations inside the canneries.

The industry anticipated that the 1981 salmon season would be short, and a number of canneries cut back on their crews. The previous winter, the Peter Pan Seafoods cannery at False Pass, Alaska burned to the ground. Peter Pan also decided not to reopen the Squaw Harbor cannery for the summer and instead expanded

2 union officials shot, 1 fatally

by Tomas Guillen
Times staff reporter

A cannery-union officer was killed and another critically wounded yesterday by two men who walked into the union's headquarters in Pioneer Square and gunned them down.

The slain man was identified as Gene Viernes, 29, the union dispatcher, and the wounded man as Silme Domingo, 29, the secretary-treasurer.

Three months ago, Rodolfo P. Nazario — the union's dispatcher before Viernes defeated him in an election in September — was slain in the parking lot of the apartment where he lived at 5031 Empire Way S.

Nazario was shot at least four times at close range about 9:30 p.m. March 5 as he left his apartment to make a telephone call. The slaying remains unsolved.

Last night, investigators were attempting to determine if the slayings were connected because both the same union and held the ...

In yesterday's sho... scene. He suffer... the che... M...

went out to get a breath of fresh air and saw Domingo crawling on the sidewalk near the office entrance.

"I looked over and the guy looked like a drunk. But then I saw all the blood on his stomach," said Holm. "He was waving his arms and saying: 'Can't you see me? Help me.'"

Holly Jenzen, 21, another Swannie's employee, said she was in the restaurant when she heard someone calling for help and saw the man holding his left side with his hand.

Police Capt. Mike Slessman said that when Domingo crawled out to the sidewalk the driver of a Metro Transit bus parked nearby called police.

Before Domingo was taken to surgery, he ... investigators the names of two men, Slessm... The two men were being sought.

Both the victims and the su... be Filipinos. The two union offi... in Seattle's Filipino comm...

A member of the ... did not want his n... union office...

Slime Domingo

its operations at other canneries. Meanwhile, other cannery companies announced that they would be hiring smaller crews at the Diamond E plant at Egegik and Wards Cove plants at Port Bailey, Kenai and Alitak.

At about 4:35 P.M., Pompeyo "Ben" Guloy and Jimmy Bulosan Ramil, two members of the Tulisan gang, made their way into the ILWU Local 37 union hall and gunned down Domingo and Viernes as they were finishing up their work for the day. Viernes was shot twice in the back and died in the hall. Domingo was shot four times in the abdomen. Witnesses saw Tony Dictado, leader of the Tulisan gang, driving the getaway car, a black Pontiac Trans Am with a firebird decal on the hood.

Domingo, bleeding profusely, chased the gunmen but collapsed on the sidewalk. A cook at Swannie's Restaurant & Bar across the street from the union hall spotted him and summoned help from the nearby fire sta-

Dispatching continued just days after the murders.
Tom Barlet photo. Courtesy Seattle Post-Intelligencer.

tion. Before he lost consciousness, Domingo told a paramedic that Guloy and Ramil were the ones who shot him. The paramedic wrote the names down. Domingo was transported to Harborview Medical Center, where he underwent three surgeries for his wounds. He regained consciousness during the night and again the next morning, when he tried to relate what had happened. But his heart finally gave out, and he passed away at the hospital twenty-four hours after he was shot.

Holding Fast inside the Union

Within days of the murders, the grieving and stunned members of the Rank-and-File Committee regrouped to figure out what to do. The Local 37 executive board decided to appoint Silme's younger sister, Lynn, to take his place as secretary-treasurer. It also created a four-member dispatch team—David Della, Angel Doniego, John Foz, and Alonzo Suson—hoping to reduce the danger to any one individual. "We made sure that no one was ever left alone in the hall again," Mast said.

The murders traumatized the community and changed the lives of friends and family forever. They also further divided the Filipino community, already polarized over heated disagreements between longtime supporters of Marcos and reformers who pushed for an aggressive program of changes at the Filipino Community of Seattle. Members and supporters of the Union of Democratic Filipinos who had been working directly with Domingo and Viernes were in shock but demonstrated their staunch loyalty to the two slain men by continuing to fight for change.

Several hours before the murders, Doniego visited the union hall to meet with Domingo and tell him that he would be resigning from the Local 37 board. He had been offered a job as a disc jockey at a country-and-western station in Arizona. Doniego, a streetwise activist with combat experience in Vietnam, knew some of the Tulisan gang members, including

From left, Mila DeGuzman, Celia Rodriguez, Terri Mast, Cindy Domingo, Leni Marin, and Cathi Tactaquin. Despite overwhelming grief, the reformers persevered in efforts to institute union reform. *Dean Wong photo.*

one of the triggermen, Ben Guloy. He was so profoundly affected by the murders that he turned down the Arizona opportunity and stayed to help provide security for the badly shaken reformers. He made this decision despite rumors the Tulisan gang had a contract out on his life. If it came to it, he was willing to risk his own life to protect the others.

Local 37 reformers David Della and Alonzo Suson were employed as clerks at Seafirst Bank at the time of the murders. On the afternoon of June 1, Della, one of Viernes's housemates, was scheduled to meet Domingo and Viernes at the union hall but was running late and got caught in traffic. The short delay may have saved him from becoming the third murder victim. Della arrived in time to help police identify Viernes, who was lying face down on the floor. "Right after the shootings, I was immediately brought in as part of the dispatch team, and then that became my full-time work," he said.

Before the murders, Suson had just made

up his mind to end his involvement with Local 37. But when he went by the office the afternoon of the murders—and saw the police barricade, Viernes's body on the floor of the union hall, and the ambulance taking Domingo off to the hospital—he was shocked. "That happened, and the next day I went to work, and I left work early. On the third day, I basically said, 'I quit. I'm back to the union office.'"

Terri Mast, who lost her partner and the father of her two young daughters, was emotionally devastated but found the inner strength to not only continue as a Rank-and-File Committee reformer in the union but assume a new public leadership role. She took over as vice president of Local 37 in December 1981. "I think the measure of good leadership is that they train other people," she said. "And so I think that that's what they underestimated when they killed Gene and Silme. They took them out, but they didn't stop the movement. I guess I felt like Gene and Silme—I could hear

continued on page 40

Elaine Ikoma Ko discusses theory behind murders.
Dean Wong photo.

The Murder Trials and the Search for Truth

At the same time that the Rank-and-File Committee rallied its members to defend its program of union reforms, those who were close to the two slain men formed the Committee for Justice for Domingo and Viernes, which supported aggressive criminal prosecution of those who perpetrated the murders. The committee held its first public meeting on June 22, 1981 at the union hall. The initial co-chairs of the steering committee were Silme's brother, Nemesio Domingo, Jr., and Elaine Ikoma Ko. The Committee for Justice published a newsletter providing updates on the progress of the murder cases and worked with the King County Prosecutor's Office to follow all potential leads.

Ikoma Ko, executive director of the International District Housing Alliance at the time, served as a principal spokesperson for the group, which met at various locations in the International District and in individual homes. "We were all there when the murders happened, and so the Committee for Justice kind of evolved organically," she recalled. "We were committed because we were all part of the same movement. These were families you've known all your life, and our camaraderie went very deep. It was a very intense time. It was all-consuming. We had meetings that would go on all night. But we wanted to make sure Silme and Gene got full justice."

On September 24, 1981, Ben Guloy, twenty-two, and Jimmy Ramil, twenty-nine, were convicted of two counts of aggravated first-degree murder after a six-week trial before King County Superior Court Judge Lloyd

Cindy Domingo was co-chair of the Committee for Justice for Domingo and Viernes steering committee. *Dean Wong photo.*

Bever. King County senior deputy prosecutor Joanne Maida argued that the two members of the Tulisan gang committed the murders because Viernes and Domingo—in creating a new dispatch system based on seniority instead of bribes—disrupted gambling operations in Alaska, which had yielded profits for Tulisan gang members who served as enforcers during the games.

A key witness in the case was Robert San Pablo, foreman of the Peter Pan cannery in Dillingham, Alaska, who testified that the head of the Tulisan gang, Fortunato "Tony" Dictado, threatened to kill Viernes because Viernes had refused to dispatch Tulisan members to Alaska. San Pablo said that Dictado made the threat at a Chinese restaurant in the International District the day before the mur-

ders. Both Guloy and Ramil were sentenced to life in prison without the possibility of parole.

The following year, Dictado, twenty-nine, was found guilty of two counts of aggravated first-degree murder in a trial that replayed much of the testimony from the earlier trial. Senior deputy prosecutor Joanne Maida, arguing this time before a jury in the courtroom of Superior Court Judge Terrance Carroll, said that Dictado was the one who ordered the murders of Domingo and Viernes. The jury convicted him on May 12, 1982. On August 20, 1982, Judge Carroll sentenced Dictado to life in prison without the possibility of parole.

Although Local 37 president Tony Baruso was arrested six weeks after the murders when law enforcement discovered that the murder weapon was registered in his name, he was released for lack of other evidence tying him to the murders. Baruso claimed that the gun, a .45 caliber Mac-10 submachine gun, had been stolen from him. However, during the trials of Guloy, Ramil, and Dictado, he refused to answer questions about his connections to the murders, the weapon, or the Tulisan gang, invoking his Fifth Amendment right against self-incrimination. During the trial of Guloy and Ramil, he invoked the Fifth Amendment 109 times; during Dictado's trial, he invoked it 31 times.

Even after the convictions of Guloy, Ramil, and Dictado, the Committee for Justice remained dogged in its pursuit of the full truth. Its members continued to urge the King County prosecutor to charge Baruso with murder, believing he had a direct hand in the murders and that he was the link to others higher

up—not yet revealed—who may have had reasons to eliminate Viernes and Domingo. They noted that Baruso, who often boasted of his strong support of Ferdinand Marcos, might have a political reason for wanting the two activists out of the way.

On November 20, 1989, after years of diligent investigation, a wrongful death civil suit charging the Marcos regime with complicity in the murders went to trial in federal district court in Seattle before Judge Barbara Rothstein. According to attorneys for the Domingo and Viernes families, the two men were murdered because of their outspoken opposition to the repression of the Marcos regime. Their activities, including sponsorship of a labor convention resolution calling for an investigative team to travel to the Philippines, brought them into "a headlong collision" with the re-

Tony Baruso, March 1991.
Kamol Sudthayakorn photo. Courtesy International Examiner.

gime's surveillance network in the United States, the attorneys contended.

During the trial, Jeff Robinson, attorney for the plaintiffs, argued that on May 17, 1981, the sum of $15,000 was paid out of the Mabuhay Corporation, an "intelligence slush fund" set up by Dr. Leonilo Malabed, a close ally of President Marcos, for a "special security project." The money, Robinson argued, went directly to Tony Baruso to pay for the murders. When Baruso took the stand as a hostile witness on December 5, 1989, he invoked the Fifth Amendment seventy-five times.

Michael Withey, attorney for the Domingo and Viernes families, interviewed Marcos in his Honolulu beach house in July 1986 and May 1987 for the trial. Marcos, who fled the Philippines in 1986 when his brutal regime collapsed, died on September 28, 1989, shortly before the civil suit came to trial. But the videotape of the interviews was played in the courtroom. Marcos claimed little knowledge of intelligence efforts against U.S.-based opponents to his regime. "I have never heard of any serious effort to infiltrate an anti-Marcos organization in the United States," he said. Marcos also invoked the Fifth Amendment in response to questions about the Mabuhay Corporation, claiming that right under both the Philippine and the U.S. Constitution.

Attorney Robinson read from an interview with former Philippine first lady Imelda Marcos, also named as a defendant in the suit. She claimed that she had lost contact with Malabed and that she had never heard of Domingo or Viernes.

On December 15, 1989 the six-member federal jury found Marcos liable for the murders and awarded $15.1 million in damages to the Domingo and Viernes families. On January 12, 1990, Judge Rothstein handed down additional liability judgments against Baruso and Malabed, awarding an additional $8.4 million to the victims' families. Later rulings reduced the final settlement to $2 million. The Marcoses' assets were frozen in 1986 after the Philippine government sued them for the re-turn of billions allegedly hidden in secret bank accounts in Switzerland and elsewhere. A U.S. district court judge in Los Angeles approved the settlement on May 20, 1991.

The participation of a foreign government in the murders of two American citizens was an "extraordinary" move that the young activists would never have envisioned, according to Bruce Occena. Fortunately, he said, the Marcoses were at least held accountable for their actions, even though the human cost was immense and justice was slow in coming. "When you go to law school, they use this case," he said. "Here's a case where a foreign government was held liable for the murder of United States citizens."

Meanwhile, on the heels of the successful civil suit, the King County Prosecutor's Office decided to take action against Baruso. In 1991, nearly ten years after the murders of Domingo and Viernes, the authorities brought murder charges against Baruso, armed now with a second motive and a new piece of evidence from the 1989 civil suit against the Marcoses.

During the earlier trials, the stated motive for the murders was that Domingo and Viernes were involved in union reform that had disrupted gambling operations in Alaska. The new motive was that the two men were silenced because of their outspoken opposition to the Marcos dictatorship in the Philippines. The new piece of evidence was the payment of $15,000 to Baruso from Malabed. On March 8, 1991, however, in an unusual decision, the King County Superior Court jury found Baruso liable for only one count of aggravated first-degree murder, believing that he caused the death of Viernes but not of Domingo. The jury was not convinced of the second motive—that the two were murdered because of a larger international conspiracy to silence the two Marcos opponents—but believed there was sufficient evidence to show that Baruso wanted Viernes murdered. On the strength of the one murder count, Baruso was given a life sentence without the possibility of parole.

1982-1984 ILWU Local 37 officers and executive board. Back row (from left) David Della, Emily Van Bronkhorst, Nemesio Domingo, Sr., John Foz, Alonzo Suson. Middle row (from left) Rich Gurtiza, Sammy Reyes, Lynn Domingo, Bernardo Taclay, Ricardo Farinas, Jr. Front row (from left) Emma Catague, Terri Mast, Leo Lorenzo, Myrna Bumanlag, Sharon Lind.
John Stamets photo.

continued from page 35
them in me saying, 'Okay, this is your time.'"

There were occasions when Mast, unaccustomed to public speaking and writing, drew inspiration from the voices of Domingo and Viernes, urging her on. "Sometimes it will just start flowing, and I know it's not necessarily my voice," she said. "It's a different voice speaking inside." She also heard the sound of Domingo's footsteps coming up the stairs at night, even after the murders. "We lived in that apartment, and we lived on the third floor. There were metal steps going up. And he used to wear those big platform shoes."

Bruce Occena said that if there are heroes in the story of Silme Domingo and Gene Viernes, it was the folks on the front line of the reform efforts who, despite their devastating grief after the murders, mustered the collective strength and fortitude to "go back in and turn the key and open up the union and get ready for the next dispatch."

"I really hate to think—if we had collapsed the way the people who murdered Gene and Silme thought we would—where we'd be today," he said. "It would just be a human tragedy. That's not what happened. We were back at that union the next morning. The blood was barely dry, and so it was stunning that we went back there."

The reformers were fearful of the Tulisan gang members who continued to be involved in the union and uncertain about who else might have been involved in the murders. In the months that followed, the gang members would circle the union hall in their cars, park outside, and watch the reformers. "We'd get strange phone calls at home all times of the day and night," Mast said. The union installed bulletproof glass in the union hall and even issued bulletproof vests to its leaders, cautioning them to travel in groups.

For Mast, a huge personal challenge was how to raise her two daughters as a single parent while continuing the work of the union and attending meetings of the newly formed Committee for Justice for Domingo and Viernes, meetings that frequently stretched into the night. Fortunately, she had the support of her parents. Emily Van Bronkhorst lived with Mast for a time to help out financially. "Sometimes, I look back and I just go, 'I don't know how I did it sometimes.'" she remarked. Her worst fear was that her young girls might be harmed in some way. "It's the kind of terror I never want to live through again," she said. "I would ride home with my kids, convinced that my car was rigged to blow up at any second."

Almost immediately, suspicion centered on Tony Baruso because of his opposition to the Rank-and-File Committee reforms. The reformers monitored Baruso's movements in and out of the union after the murders and took note of the people he met with. Later that year, the murder weapon was recovered in a Seattle city park and was found to be registered to Baruso, but it was years before enough evidence surfaced to bring criminal charges against him.

Because Baruso wielded so much power in the union and in the community, the activists had been reluctant to speak out against him and even held back from challenging him for his post in both the 1978 and 1980 union elections. But a key moment came at a special union meeting within a week of the murders when Baruso tried to claim that he had given his support and blessing to Domingo's and Viernes's reform efforts. As Baruso spoke, Tulisan gang members stood along the wall, observing

Looking at 1982 election results. From left, Angel Doniego, Jack Buenavista, Toribio Martin, and John Foz. *Greg Tuai photo. Courtesy* International Examiner.

the proceedings. Mast, aware that ILWU International secretary-treasurer Curtis McClain was in the room, overcame her fear, moved to the front of the room, and challenged his statement. "I was infuriated," she said. "I stood up and said, 'Let's be clear about this. Don't talk as if you supported Gene and Silme's efforts, because you didn't. And this was their work, not yours.'" After Mast spoke, there was silence and then thunderous applause from the union members. "When we saw that, it helped push us together," Suson recalled.

Baruso, who had served as Local 37 president since 1975, lost a recall election on December 4, 1981, after Mast discovered evidence that he had submitted forged ballots on behalf of Local 37 workers in the most recent election of ILWU International officers. Following his ouster, a U.S. Labor Department audit

of union records revealed numerous financial abuses by Baruso. On July 28, 1982, ILWU Local 37 filed a civil suit against Baruso on the basis of this audit. In 1984, following a five-day trial before U.S. District judge Jack Tanner in Tacoma, Baruso was convicted of embezzlement, committing mail fraud, and filing false records. Witnesses testified that Baruso embezzled union funds through double payments. He was sentenced to three years in prison and ordered to pay back more than $5,600 to Local 37.

With Baruso gone, the door was open to full reform of the union. In the 1982 elections, the Rank-and-File Committee swept all the positions. Terri Mast became president, and Leo Lorenzo, a union pioneer, was elected vice president. David Della won the position of secretary-treasurer, and Alonzo Suson was

(From left) Bernardo Taclay, David Della, Nemesio Domingo, Sr. (seated), and Terri Mast (far right).
IBU, Region 37 collection.

PART 1. THE ERA

chosen dispatcher. The reformers took all the trustee and member-at-large positions as well, enabling them to implement the reforms they had worked so hard to put into place.

Finding the Way Forward in a Changing Industry

For the Rank-and-File Committee reformers, achieving power in ILWU Local 37 turned out to be a mixed blessing. They were at last able to bring a renewed sense of purpose, fairness and a strong sense of democracy to a union that had wavered from the defining values that first brought it into being in the 1930s.

But the activists achieved power just as they lost two of their strongest leaders and the public image of the union had been tarnished by the murders. In that environment and under those circumstances, it was hard to make progress. Van Bronkhorst recalled going to Alaska with Suson immediately after the murders to organize workers in Dutch Harbor and bring them into Local 37. "There was no opportunity to win that election," she said. "The companies put up articles in the papers everywhere—'Union leaders slain in Seattle union hall. Cannery worker leaders murdered. Thugs in Seattle.' They put that everywhere."

In 1982, Della and Van Bronkhorst tried to organize at the Trident Seafoods plant in Dutch Harbor. Again, they were unsuccessful. In 1984, they trekked up to Seward Fisheries in Homer and to canneries on the Kenai Peninsula. Again, they failed. "We couldn't get the majority of people to sign up for the election," Della said.

Companies capitalizing on the union's troubled image weren't the only reason for Local 37's inability to expand union representation; the union's difficulties were a reflection of a profound shift in the political climate and a changing industry. Many companies had merged or simply closed up shop, resulting in fewer union jobs. In 1983, the Ocean Beauty Seafoods facility in Uganik Bay was sold, and Diamond E Fisheries declared bankruptcy.

Meanwhile, some canneries shifted their production into fresh-frozen and cut the number of workers on the canning lines.

At its height, Local 37 dispatched more than 5,000 members to fifty canneries. By 1983, the dispatch total had fallen to 765, with the loss that year of three hundred jobs from Egegik, Chugach, and Uganik Bay. By the mid-1980s, as the industry shifted its production, Local 37 expanded its jurisdiction to include shellfish processing and fresh-frozen products and represented cannery, cold-storage, fresh-frozen, and salmon-roe workers.

In 1986, poor salmon runs, coupled with the steady shift from canned to fresh-frozen processing, resulted in the closure of the Columbia Wards Fisheries plant at Kenai. In that same year, Peter Pan Seafoods closed its Dillingham plant.

Because of tight finances, Suson and Van Bronkhorst left for jobs in other unions. Suson departed around 1987 after the disappointing election losses, looking "to find some work stability." He joined the International District Housing Alliance as a community organizer and later moved on to hone his collective bargaining skills at the Hotel Employees & Restaurant Employees Local 8 and later at the Service Employees International Union. For a time, Mast and Della were the two key individuals holding Local 37 together.

The decline of Local 37 was not an isolated phenomenon. It mirrored a national decline in the strength of the labor movement as the country began a rightward turn under the fiercely antiunion Reagan administration. In 1981, President Reagan fired thirteen thousand air traffic controllers who had gone on strike for better working conditions and better pay, destroying their union. That move set the stage for the coming years, when private companies began pushing back against worker protections and refused to enter into collective bargaining agreements.

In February 1986, Mast and other Local 37 leaders decided to move out of the union hall in the Pioneer Square neighborhood. The structure, built on filled tideland, had become unsafe as the floor began to sink and bricks fell

Following the murders, Emily Van Bronkhorst and Alonzo Suson continued to organize in Alaska, but found it difficult to make headway in the changing political climate.
John Stamets photo.

Proud of the achievements of the early *manong* pioneers, ILWU Local 37 members organize a celebration in 1984 to recognize those who had participated in the union for over 25 years.
Skip Kerr photo. Courtesy International Examiner.

out of the basement wall. The cost of stabilizing the structure was prohibitive. The union, which had occupied the building since 1947, moved temporarily to the Labor Temple in downtown Seattle. At the time, Mast said, the decision to move, made at a February membership meeting, was "real difficult" because many union pioneers had put their toil and hearts into developing the union hall.

Finally, in 1987, Local 37 found a more stable home when it merged with the Inlandboatmen's Union, the marine division of the ILWU, and became Region 37 of the IBU. The merger with a larger, stronger body helped strengthen Local 37's bargaining position for upcoming contract negotiations and stabilize union finances. It also brought an important new connection because the IBU represents workers who operate the tugs that transport seafood to the processing plants.

Since the merger, the companies that were the target of the class action discrimination lawsuits have gone out of business. In 2002, Wards Cove Packing Company announced that it was shutting down all nine of its salmon-processing plants, including the original Wards Cove cannery, which opened in 1928. The one remaining employer was Peter Pan Seafoods; it was never a part of the lawsuits and had a very different policy on how it treated its employees. Many of the plants that remain open today have converted to freezing rather than canning operations.

During the merger, Mast became the regional director of Region 37. In 1993, she was elected national secretary-treasurer for the Inlandboatmen's Union, the position she holds today. Rich Gurtiza replaced her as regional director and continues in that post.

Changing Tides

Today, there are still many unorganized workers in Alaska, toiling with limited protections in remote workplaces. In the United States, the percentage of organized workers in the private sector is in decline, down to 7 percent. When Local 37 reformers were organizing in Alaska in the 1970s and 1980s, 18 to 20 percent of all U.S. workers were unionized.

Region 37 of the Inlandboatmen's Union continues to represent about a thousand members. The seafood industry has gone through many changes in the past thirty years, moving away from canned to fresh-frozen products, which are less labor-intensive and sold mostly on the foreign market. The industry is also challenged by competition from farm-raised fish from Canada, Chile, and Europe. By the early 1990s, the aquaculture industry had captured a substantial share of the salmon market, and by 2009, farm-raised fish accounted for half of the fish consumed globally.

Gone are the small wooden fishing boats of the past. Now, massive factory trawlers harvest huge quantities of fish. These vessels, many of which are converted oil vessels, catch, clean, and freeze the fish in large processing plants below the trawl deck. Industry representatives say the sixty-odd factory trawlers and their supporting industries employ more than 6,500 people. Nearly all factory trawlers are headquartered in Seattle. Most do not employ unionized laborers.

Organizing workers is increasingly difficult because union officials are rarely allowed to enter these workplaces, and special legislation has allowed factory ships to escape labor laws that apply to shore plants. "Who wants to mention the word 'union' and end up treading water in the Bering Sea?" the *Alaskero News* asked. "Some processing outfits outrageously exploit the entire industry's reputation and its overall quality and stability by relying on cheap, inexperienced and poorly motivated 'throw-away labor.'"

As the salmon-canning industry has declined as a U.S. domestic industry, some of the salmon are transported to and processed in other countries, such as Thailand and Mexico, where labor is cheaper. The canned or packed fish is sold on the international market.

In 1978, Gene Viernes presaged this change in his article in the *International Examiner*, "The Passing of the Alaskeros." He noted that after one hundred years, the annual migration of workers from the lower forty-eight states was nearing an end because of drastic cutbacks in jobs caused by the shift from canned-salmon production to fresh-frozen fish processed on mechanized bottom fishing plants. He predicted that these plants, operated nearly year-round by foreign firms, will eventually run on skeleton crews of low-paid workers. "In the future, factories will have maintenance machinists, and just a few laborers who will glaze the fish and send the precious product to the freezers," Viernes wrote. "Or, in the case of bottom fishing, the laborers will turn the machine on and off."

Today, the Alaskeros who made up a substantial majority of the workforce are mostly a remnant of the past. Latinos, Vietnamese immigrants, and college students now make up the union's diminished membership.

Abandoned canneries still dot Alaska's shoreline, slowly succumbing to the effects of time and weather. However, these dramatic sites are attracting new interest. In July 2004, developers converted a shuttered Wards Cove Packing Company cannery on the Kenai River into a historic and artistic attraction, touting its warehouses, bunkhouses, and antique machinery as offering visitors a view of how a salmon cannery once operated.

In 2006, Terri Mast took her daughters on a trip to several canneries in Alaska, including the Peter Pan facility in Dillingham, still in operation, and the converted Wards Cove facility. She said she loved explaining the salmon-canning process to her daughters: "But I did feel a bit melancholy because of all that had happened, and I hadn't been up to the canneries since 1993. It was putting an end to some things for me.

"It was sort of odd to see the Wards Cove facility remade into a tourist destination," she added. "I remember how vibrant it used to be up there. It made me sad to see that. But to their credit, there were plaques and signs that showed the segregated bunkhouses and explaining the Iron Chink. It's a good thing that they didn't tear the cannery down."

One Generation's Time

Most of the organizers who worked alongside Viernes and Domingo and those who stepped into the gap after the murders have continued as activists. But many moved on to other pursuits after the corruption was rooted out of the union and jobs in Alaska became scarce.

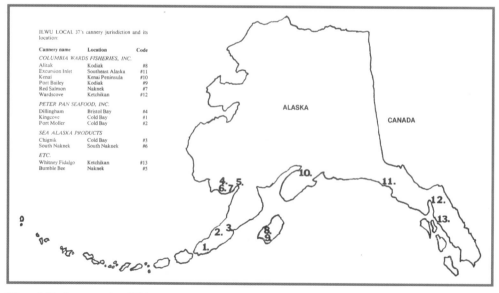

Map of Alaska canneries, 1983.
Alaskero News. *IBU, Region 37 collection.*

(From left) Terri Mast, Rich Gurtiza, John Foz, and David Della.
Dean Wong photo.

After a lifetime of low-paid community activism, many of these aging reformers find themselves still working full-time, trying to make ends meet. Others are attempting to ease into retirement. Meanwhile, another generation of young community organizers, motivated by the same passion for peace and social justice that drove their predecessors, seeks out these veteran activists, mining them for their knowledge and wisdom just as Viernes and Domingo did with the *manong* pioneer reformers of Local 37.

As the baton is passed, the reformers wonder what is of most value to be shared between generations. Has the advent of the Internet and social media made the face-to-face organizing strategies of the past obsolete? As the political winds shift rightward in the United States, how do today's organizers build momentum, sustain their spirit, and find the resources to support their work?

Rich Gurtiza, who remained with Local 37 and the Inlandboatmen's Union for many years after the murders, said that as long as there are vulnerable workers, there is a need for an organization to represent them. "When somebody goes into organizing, it is not for themselves, but it's for others," he said. "If you want to go and try to make a bunch of money, then this isn't the place for you." The rewards are spiritual, he explained, "and how you feel about yourself."

Terri Mast believes that labor organizing is even more urgently needed during the current economic recession than it was thirty years ago. "There's a lot of fear and intimidation in this country around workers' ability to organize, and employers use it all the time," she said. "I think the opportunity to organize is there, but I think also labor has to reach out to young workers and help them understand the history, because I think we've fallen down a bit on that."

John Foz contends that the basics of organizing are still the same: training shop stewards, forming safety committees, and educating workers about their rights. But he points to the current challenge of organizing during a political lull. During the 1960s and 1970s, he noted, students were taking to the streets in active protest against the Vietnam War, and it was a political climate more conducive to organizing efforts.

Michael Woo recalls how Silme Domingo emphasized the importance of understanding—and adapting to—the natural ebb and flow of organizing work. "Where he got that from, I don't know," said Woo. "It became part of our organizing strategy. When times are good, that's when things are flowing. Then you need to be doing more of the organizing. Because when times are bad—the ebb—if people are organized, you're more ready to take action. If no one's been doing the organizing, when the ebb hits like now, there's no critical mass of politicized, skilled leaders to move a movement. Silme was so right."

Emma Catague said that one lesson she passes on to young activists is to be direct and passionate but also to be patient in cultivating community relationships. "You cannot go in there like you're gung-ho, like, 'Oh, I know it all.' It's not going to work." Pushing their agenda as if they are the experts will not fly, she tells them.

Alonzo Suson, who now organizes in Dhaka, Bangladesh, and for the past six years in Cambodia, said his advice to young organizers is to not simply take action but also to study their work and reflect, have discussions with peers, and learn through the constant exchange of ideas.

Still Haunted by Memory

Silme Domingo and Gene Viernes believed—as most activists of their generation did—that if social change was to come to the United States, it had to come from many people pooling their efforts and forming a collective voice of defiance against the status quo. What gave them hope and courage was rediscovering stories about the raw perseverance of the Asian American pioneers who came before them, who never gave up. They were sustained along the way by the patient support of their families, especially their siblings, with whom they could share thoughts and ideas as they discovered their voices in the hopeful milieu of the era in which they lived.

Andy Pascua said a significant lesson from that time was the importance of education in spurring institutional change. "It wasn't changing the owners of the factories," Pascua said. "It wasn't changing a corrupt union leader, because in the future, there could be another one. You had to change the whole institution, how you dispatched, how you enforced contracts. The whole system had to be changed. In order to change that, you have to educate whole groups of people."

The murders reverberated most deeply inside the families who lost their loved ones. Silme Domingo and Gene Viernes were emotional anchors and role models for those around them, especially their younger siblings. Regardless of how busy they became—and the organizing work often became all-consuming—they always made time to spend with their families and friends.

Viernes, who began living in Seattle during his years of work on the ACWA lawsuits and union reform efforts, regularly made the two-and-a-half-hour drive back to Wapato, the community that had nurtured him in the beginning and remained his first home. He became the guiding force in the family after their father passed away suddenly from a heart attack on New Year's Eve, 1972. He took care of and helped support his widowed mother and younger siblings.

His younger brothers, Stan and Steve, were also young Alaskeros. Stan began going to Alaska in 1969, two years after Gene; Steve started in 1978.

Even from a very early age, Viernes pushed Steve, six years his junior, to develop the qualifications to become a machinist in an industry that employed very few nonwhites in those higher-paying positions. From the sixth grade, Steve said, Gene began to teach him about

Silme Domingo's sister, Lynn, described him as both a protective older brother and a political mentor. Lynn attended Blanchet High School, where she was one of only five minority students. "He would make sure that I was a good kid and that I was protected and I had a ride," she said. "I didn't even have a date for the prom, so he made sure I had a date for the prom. He also taught me how to drink tequila."

She observed her brother's way of doing community organizing, how he relished the opportunity to develop relationships and work with young people. "Silme was really out there, really social," she commented. In contrast, Lynn said, she was very different, having a stronger interest in art, cooking, and "being at home." It was because of Silme's influence that she learned how to become an activist.

The sudden loss of her beloved older brother when she was only twenty-two filled her with grief. She was also consumed with anger at the perpetrators and distrusted government. "It was very, very difficult," she said. "I cried every day, and I think I even tried committing suicide at one point." To this day, she has not stopped grieving. Her sorrow was lightened only a bit when she heard that Tony Baruso had died in 2008 in Stafford Creek Prison near Aberdeen, Washington.

all kinds of "mechanical things," whether it was rebuilding cars or rewiring the house—skills that came into play later in his career. "We used to make our parents pretty mad at us because we were always tearing something apart," Steve said. With Gene's brotherly coaxing, Steve broke through a major barrier when he became a machinist year-round in the canneries, overhauling, fixing, and maintaining equipment.

Stan Viernes was so deeply affected by his brother's murder that he was catatonic for days. Stan called Gene "my role model, my beacon in life. My wife was saying the biggest thing is that it's really hard for us that he wasn't around to watch my kids grow up, just the way my dad wasn't around. The other day, my wife told me that she'd just like to hear my brother Gene's voice, just to have the connection." But they've accepted that Gene is gone. "He's part of history," he said. "We have to share him with everybody else."

Others who were not Viernes and Domingo family members were also devastated by the murders. Angel Doniego spent much of his young life on the street to escape an abusive home life, and Domingo's death affected him profoundly. "This was the first time I ever cried in my life since I left the Philippines," Doniego said. In addition to the political work they did together, he and Domingo enjoyed crazy, fun times sitting under the freeway, drinking tequila and smoking pot. "In the war in Vietnam, I never cried," Doniego said.

"I didn't have any feelings at all. I could cut that off. But this was different. Silme was like a brother to me. That's why I loved him so much. So you lose somebody like that, it just kind of blew me away."

Both Andy Pascua and Rich Gurtiza were inspired by Viernes, yet they were haunted because they had known him so well. Gurtiza said that for nearly ten years, he gauged his accomplishments against Gene's unflinching commitment, never feeling like he could quite measure up. He only recently realized that he was chasing an impossible goal. Pascua likewise says that Viernes's memory "throws a big shadow." Sometimes when he is working and feels tired and doesn't want to fight the bureaucracy, he remembers the magnitude of Viernes's and Domingo's sacrifice: "You know, Gene and Silme were killed, and I'm worried [somebody's] going to yell at me?" He went on, "When you're a young man, you have the energy, and you're strong and you're committed. When you're an old man, sometimes you just want to sit on the couch. You don't want to fight with them. You don't want to, but the standard is there. And so I think, What do I do? Do I not believe who we were, who we are? And if I won't maintain those standards, then maybe we weren't who I think we were."

In those private moments, Gene Viernes and Silme Domingo continue to inspire in those who knew them the fiery idealism that made the Civil Rights Era a bright and optimistic time. That spirit of commitment comes from the shared experience of fighting for change but learning that change doesn't come overnight, that the struggle for progress is slow and unremitting.

Viernes and Domingo were trailblazers in a generation that yielded many pioneers, each person striving—in his or her own way, within individual spheres of interest—to break down barriers to equality and justice. Many of the activists who worked with them have moved on and made a difference in other arenas beyond the salmon canneries where they got their start.

Pascua points out that many children of the Alaskeros became the first Asian Americans in their chosen fields simply because certain arenas had been closed to their parents' generation. He said that when he took a job at the Washington State Department of Social and Health Services as a Child Protective Services caseworker, he became the first Filipino American dealing with child abuse issues. "Whatever you were doing in that generation, you were breaking ground simply because you were alive and you were doing your thing," Pascua remarked.

Even though Domingo and Viernes considered themselves revolutionaries, eschewing involvement in the mainstream electoral process, their work inspired friends and colleagues to step into the political process after their deaths. After the murders, Velma Veloria, an immigrant and fellow Union of Democratic Filipinos activist, moved to Seattle from New York, with the aim of helping to carry on union reform efforts. She was dispatched to work at the Peter Pan Seafoods cannery in King Cove, Alaska. Despite the initial skepticism of others in the Union of Democratic Filipinos, she chose to run for office as a way of declaring that the United States was her home. In 1992, Veloria won election to the Washington State Legislature. The first Filipina to be elected to a state legislature in the continental United States, she served for twelve years, advocating for workers' rights and social justice and coauthoring legislation to ban human trafficking.

David Della also pursued public office. He was elected to a term on the Seattle City Council in 2003 after serving as deputy chief of staff for Seattle Mayor Norm Rice and later as director of the Washington State Commission on Asian Pacific American Affairs. Della believes his working-class origins directed him toward social reform, but, he said, the murders "directed me toward public service."

"What You Leave Behind"

At the time of the murders, Domingo had two young daughters—Ligaya, three, and Kalayaan, not yet one. Viernes didn't have children, but he was the proud uncle of two-year-old Conan, the son of his brother, Stan, and Stan's wife, Gloria. Ligaya and Kalayaan both grew up in the Beacon Hill neighborhood of Seattle. Conan is a Wapato native and works as a program analyst for the University of Washington Office of Minority Affairs and Diversity in Toppenish.

Thirty years later, Ligaya and Kalayaan are following a career path similar to that of their parents—working as community organizers and social justice advocates, carrying the fight into the next generation. While this might have seemed inevitable given their upbringing, they've also made conscious choices. And their journey hasn't been easy.

During her second year of college, Ligaya wanted to drop out to become a union organizer. Even though her mother had told her that she "could be anything she wanted to be," Ligaya recalled a tearful meeting: "She said, 'I don't want you to do that. I'm afraid that something will happen to you, that you'll end up like me, without choices, and that you won't finish school.'" Ligaya kept her promise to her mother that she would complete school while she was organizing full-time.

For the Domingo girls, the reason their father was not around was too complex to explain to their peers. "It wasn't even about relating to them that my dad was dead," Kalayaan said. "It was about relating to them that this really weird thing had happened—that he was murdered, whether he was murdered by gang members or he was murdered by a union guy or he was murdered by the president of the Philippines. Every part of that story is pretty weird. And so you just sort of not talk about it. You learn not to be sad about it."

Conan's only personal memory of his Uncle Gene is of the straw backpacks from the Philippines that Viernes gave him upon returning from his 1981 trip—and a valuable early edition of the *Conan the Barbarian* comic book that Viernes brought as a gift after he was born. Conan keeps the treasured comic book in a sealed bag.

Viernes purchased the comic book after learning that Stan and Gloria had named their

(From left) Terri Mast, Stephanie Velasco, Rich Gurtiza, and James Gregory at the Domingo-Viernes Memorial Anniversary in 2011. Velasco was the first recipient of the Domingo-Viernes Scholarship. *David Groves photo. Courtesy Harry Bridges Center for Labor Studies.*

first child Conan. Emily Van Bronkhorst recalled accompanying him to a collectibles store in Seattle's Pike Place Market, where he purchased the comic book. "The price of the comic book was, like, fifty-eight dollars!" she exclaimed. "I was shocked. It was just a hell of a lot of money to spend on a first-edition comic book for a guy who basically had no money. I always thought it was very sweet because he was so excited about this baby."

Ligaya, who works as an organizer for the Service Employees International Union Local 1199, says she at first wanted to be a marine biologist. But when she began volunteering in Northern California on a campaign to clean up oil pollution in San Francisco Bay, her thinking evolved. "I started to put it together that the struggles that we were working on as environmental activists was the same as that of workers and that it was all one struggle," she said. "From that point, I started doing union activism. Obviously, I had been around that my whole life, and it came pretty naturally."

Kalayaan is employed with the YMCA and is stationed at Cleveland High School, where she is working on building a community school. "I always had a love for science and people," she said, "and so I think a natural role

for me was that I was going to be a doctor." After college, she took a job in an adult day health center that served young adults with brain injuries and elderly adults.

"I truly was interested in looking at how to keep people healthy, not just how to treat their illnesses," Kalayaan explained. Her mother instilled in her a desire not simply to help but also to create "a sense of justice" and "a community that was fair." She realized that she didn't want to become a doctor after seeing inequities in the health care system. "So instead of wanting to be part of that, I looked at it and said I wanted to actually fix that or to find an alternative to that, which I think is actually a lot of what my mom does."

Often, the full measure of a person's life is in the lingering influence he or she leaves on others. There's wisdom in the saying: "The only thing you take with you when you're gone is what you leave behind."

A new fifty-six-unit apartment complex for low-income families was built in 2004 as part of the International District Village Square II at 721 South Lane Street in Seattle. The apartments were named the Domingo-Viernes Apartments to honor the two activists' advocacy on behalf of affordable housing for

In 2011, Gene and Silme were added to the Wall of Martyrs memorial in the Philippines. *Stan Viernes photo.*

elders and immigrant families in the 1970s.

On the thirtieth anniversary of their deaths, friends, family, and supporters gathered at the University of Washington's Center for Urban Horticulture to remember Gene Viernes and Silme Domingo and reflect on the continuing struggle for social justice. At the event, the Inlandboatmen's Union, in collaboration with the Harry Bridges Center for Labor Studies at the University of Washington, awarded the first annual Domingo-Viernes Scholarship, which supports students "committed to the principles of justice and equality." Fittingly, the first recipient was Stephanie Velasco, who graduated in 2011 as valedictorian from Wapato High School.

In November 2011, Gene Viernes and Silme Domingo were added to the Wall of Martyrs memorial in Quezon City, which honors the sacrifices of those who gave their lives opposing the brutal rule of Ferdinand Marcos. Administered by the Monument of Heroes (Bantayog ng mga Bayani) Foundation, the black granite memorial is inscribed with the names of nearly two hundred activists and resistance fighters whose work helped bring about the end of the Marcos regime in 1986. Domingo and Viernes are the first Filipino Americans added to the memorial, and their inclusion is a fitting reminder of their belief in the international scope of the fight for human rights.

As time passes, it will become more difficult to remember clearly who Gene and Silme really were, as memories fade and sometimes vanish altogether. But those who knew them take comfort in the ongoing renewal of the *spirit* of justice, fairness, and hope they represented. That spirit embodies something more deep-rooted, less fleeting, still living inside those who worked alongside them. It finds a home in another generation of activists who carry on the struggle. For the present, Gene and Silme still live strongly inside the hearts of family members and friends who loved them as human beings, not simply as symbols of a worthy cause for which they gave their lives.

It is now up to those who believed, as Silme and Gene did—in a society with a level playing field and dignity for all workers—to carry on their example. The work has passed rightly now to those who choose to continue the fight for a more tolerant, just, and compassionate world. Through them, the dream—elusive though it may be—still endures as a steadfast vision of hope.

2

Reflections

"Labor cannot stand still. It must not retreat. It must go on, or go under."

—Harry Bridges

Abraham "Rami" Arditi

Rami grew up in New York and, in 1972, moved to Seattle, where he started his career at Seattle Legal Services. In 1974, he went to work at the Northwest Labor and Employment Law Office, where he became involved in the Alaska Cannery Workers Association (ACWA) lawsuits. He retired in 2007.

Silme was a real firebrand, a very kind of charismatic figure. Gene was a very, very reliable guy, very low-key. I think of the various plaintiffs in all the different cases, probably Gene devoted more of his own energies to the lawsuits. I just remember them as two unbelievably fine human beings who were tremendously well motivated, were able to galvanize the people around them, help those people act, maybe make them act and bring about reforms.

The most challenging things about pursuing the class action lawsuits were the responses from the other side and the courts. One of the explanations from the other side was that Alaska is different, and it's not measured by the same standards and practices in the lower forty-eight. That's not a very good explanation, but I always thought they were very strong cases and we prevailed on two of them. We didn't prevail on the third one.

In the Wards Cove case, basically the heart of their defense was that the companies were not discriminating against nonwhites in the higher-paying jobs. They were discriminating against whites in the lower-paying jobs. The companies hired an expert witness, an anthropologist who testified that things were the way they were because that's the way nonwhite or minority workers wanted them. And then the next day, they withdrew his testimony. You'd have to suspect that even the companies realized that it was inappropriate and, needless to

say, somewhere off the beaten track. Naturally, I was disappointed in the outcome in the Wards Cove case. I think anyone in my shoes would be. It was a time when the whole civil rights area was changing. That was a certain part of the explanation for how things came out in the Supreme Court. It was a five-four decision and we had two very vigorous dissents. Certainly, I feel bad about the outcome.

When we first started doing discrimination work, it was much different from what it is today. There were very few lawyers on the other side who had much experience with discrimination cases. Most of the people we were up against, or a lot of them, had maybe general litigation practice or corporate litigation practice, or they were just corporate lawyers. Eventually, discrimination in employment became as much a specialty for employers and unions as it was for plaintiffs. You could see a slight shift in the political winds as far as legal enforcement, in my view, in 1977. That's when I think the very beginning of it was. That came with the election of Ronald Reagan and the Reagan appointees to the various levels of the federal court and the Bush appointees. And then, it really became different.

I remember reading a headline in one of the Seattle papers. It must have been 1988. The headline was "Supreme Court Backs Whites," or something like that. It sounded like a very sort of peculiar, most crude kind of thing for a newspaper to say, but that's the way things were being played. And certainly, if you looked at that particular case that concerned the Supreme Court ruling, a case called *Patterson v. McLean Credit Union*, it was very much that way. People, conservative judges, were worried about so-called quotas, going overboard in protecting the interests of minorities and women and what not.

Emma Catague

Shortly after Emma emigrated from the Philippines, she became involved with the anti-Marcos movement in Seattle and met Silme Domingo. Because she spoke Tagalog, he approached her about going to Alaska to do organizing work. Emma is one of the founding mothers of the Asian and Pacific Islander Women and Family Safety Center.

The day that it happened, I was actually at home. Silme and I were supposed to meet that day at two o'clock. For some reason, I missed it and took the bus home. And then at four o'clock, I got a call from Ricky Farinas. He said, "Emma, look at the news. Something happened at the union." When we turned on the TV, we saw Silme and all that. So we all rushed to Harborview because we wanted to make sure. After that, I realized I was supposed to be there. So I was going through the process, like, "What would have happened if I was there? Could I have stopped the killing, or am I one of the persons that might have been killed?" Maybe I was spared. I don't know, but up to this time, I still wonder about that.

Silme was very close to my husband and me. He was actually my oldest daughter's godfather. Silme was a person that I respected even though at the time, it was in the '70s, he wore a leather jacket, driving a Monte Carlo, the platform shoes, and hair like that. But he was very close to me because he always talked to me. He always said, "Hey, Emma, I think you are good at this." He basically provided mentoring. At the time, I was a new immigrant. Who am I? You always have this self-stigma.

He always wanted to know more about immigrants. He wanted to know more about the lifestyle. And then, because I was involved in the Filipino community and because we were activists—we were anti-Marcos, and at that time, all of the Filipino leaders were pro-Marcos—we had this tension. So I always told Silme, "You guys need to change because they're complaining that you guys—how can they believe you when you smoke marijuana and you act like this?"

Silme empowered me. Maybe if I didn't meet Silme and he didn't push me to this, I probably wouldn't be where I am, become an advocate, become an activist. Because he was the one that said, "Hey, Emma, you can do that." So he personally helped me. I wonder what could have been if Silme was still alive. When I see his kids, it also makes me reflect because our families are very close.

I went up in '77 to the canneries, Diamond E Fisheries in Egegik. I heard a lot of the elders, the *manongs*, say, "Easy money, easy money." What is easy about it? Because at some point, we were working fourteen hours a day. I saw a lot of injuries. People were falling asleep on the job, they were running this machinery, and people's fingers got cut and all that. So I started to think, "Oh, my God. This is not really easy money." For all the old *manongs* that have been going there for 40, 60 years—to them, this is not just a job. It's actually a family. Because when you are there, you are basically around with everybody else 24/7 for three to four weeks. And then, you go back to Seattle.

When I was at the union hall for meetings, our secretary-treasurer, Ponce Torres, did the roll call: "Brother Baruso, Brother Domingo." And he would also say, "Brother Catague." And so Tony Baruso would say, "Brother Torres, you've got to understand, we have a sister here. It's Sister Catague, not Brother." And so they always laughed because they're not used to having a woman in there.

Being a woman and working with some pretty traditional men was hard. It was challenging, but it taught me that you have to be assertive sometimes. It taught me that I cannot be so laid-back. I think a lot of times, when you're an immigrant, you have all this, we call it, like, oppression. You take whatever. I think what happened to me is that it gave me more challenges. It made me say, "You know what?

I will show you. I will prove that you guys are wrong. We can do it."

In some ways, it helped me understand better the situation of immigrants. That is why I became the voice for immigrants, because we are not so empowered. I worked with these *manongs*. It was so hard, but I took it as a challenge. When we were doing this anti-Marcos work, passing out flyers in front of the Kokusai Theater, Trinidad Rojo came to me and said, "As a woman, you're not supposed to be on the street. You're supposed to be home, cooking food, taking care of your family. This is not

your job!" He also said, "And if you really don't like the U.S."—because we were talking about U.S. imperialism and all of that—"then you should go back to the Philippines."

I said, "If you really like Marcos, why don't you go to the Philippines? Who are you to tell me what to do?" He looked at me and he was so mad. I was, like, "Why are these people treating me like this?" They had this way of looking at women and immigrants. They had this attitude, like you cannot go beyond this level. And so it was hard for me emotionally. I think it really just made me stronger.

David Della

At age sixteen, David began working at Wards Cove Packing Company. His father, a cannery foreman, paid the union dispatcher fifty dollars to send him up. In 2003, David was elected to a term on the Seattle City Council. He is the founder of two consulting firms specializing in sustainable energy products, Growing Energy and Eco-Ready.

My first season was 1972. Most of the Filipino crew worked in the fish house. I started out as a slimer, which means that you take out all the guts and you cut off the fins and any part of the fish that the butcher machine didn't get. And then I went into working the retort line, which is you cook the salmon in the cans to keep them fresh. I spent the day pushing the load in and pulling them out, which is pretty much heavy work. And then I ended up in the warehouse, where I loaded up the boxes of the finished salmon on the trucks and on the boats.

When I was at the cannery, I saw a lot of things that were really quite disturbing, things that you wouldn't think happened, such as a segregated bunkhouse, segregated jobs. You're stuck in certain jobs without any chance of promotion. Everything was segregated—your laundry, your mail, where you lived, the type of food you had. The bunkhouse that housed the white workers had better food. They had ice cream. We had to carry our own salted barrels of meat from the boat to our kitchen. That stuff was pretty disturbing.

We were part of a generation that started to raise questions of the company, about why is it like this, because many of our fathers and uncles before us, they just took the abuse because they had no choice. We felt we had a choice, so we started making some noise about that. When I came back, the younger people in the union were starting to talk about doing some sort of documentation of the discrimination up in Alaska to file lawsuits against the

industry. I was a plaintiff, a class member, for one of the lawsuits. I was part of the Wards Cove Packing Company class action lawsuit, so I took part in some of the documentation and earlier meetings to lay the basis for the lawsuits that were filed.

My dad thought I was a troublemaker. He was part of a generation, you know, "We had no choice. This is the industry that put food on our table, and how dare you start to question what they're doing? It's going to impact all of us." He reacted very badly about it because by that time, he was a company foreman for the Filipino crew. He was in this position where he felt like we were also targeting him. He took it very personally.

By the time he passed away, we had bridged our differences. Actually, when we marched for housing in Chinatown, my dad was one of the older guys with the bullhorns. You see him in pictures. So we kind of bridged our relationship around some of that. I talked to him about the connection between how he was feeling, having faced so much discrimination in his life here, and why it was important to bridge out to the Philippines. The problem was that he came from the same area of the country as Marcos, so he was very much a Marcos supporter. The lodge he was in, Tony Baruso was part of the lodge. He thought that Marcos did a good thing because he built roads in the Philippines. But when he realized that there was a link between that and what he was experiencing here with discrimination, he began to see the broader picture.

I was supposed to meet with Silme and Gene the day they were murdered. The meeting was set for I think four o'clock or four fifteen. Well, I was running late from work, and I was caught in traffic. I was coming down Second Avenue. Silme always parked his car on the corner in front of the union hall. The hall was cordoned off, and there were police cars and fire trucks there. So I went around the block and parked somewhere, and I walked up to the union hall. People were standing around, and I was met by a police officer standing outside, saying, "You can't go in here. There was a shooting in here." I said, "Shooting?" He said, "Yes. Two people got shot. We think it might be a gang thing, and one person was taken to the hospital." I said, "Well, I'm a union member, and I'm late for a meeting here." He said, "Who are you meeting with?" I said, "I'm meeting with Silme Domingo and Gene Viernes." He said, "Well, those are the two guys who were shot. One of them is in here, and we need somebody to identify him."

So I went in there. They took me inside. He was on the floor, and I said, "That's Gene Viernes. He's my roommate. Where's Silme Domingo, because his car is on the corner." Well, they took him to the hospital. So then, the police took me up to Harborview where Silme was. I got up there, and he was in surgery. I made phone calls from the hospital to everyone about what had happened, that the shooting had occurred. I went back down to the union hall after that. Gene was still there, and we helped clean up and put him in a body bag. We made phone calls from across the street at Swannie's Restaurant & Bar to tell people what was going on. It's kind of a blur from there. From the moment I got there, it was all just kind of a fog. It was very surreal.

Immediately after the shootings, we knew we had to continue the work because we knew that it was an intentional shooting. It wasn't just a random kind of thing, right? We knew that it was intentional because of the work that we were doing. We formed a dispatch team. We were going to consult with the then-president Baruso about what we were doing, but we were essentially going to take over and continue with the reform. It had a great effect on the rank-and-file movement, which in a very accelerated way, notched it up pretty much. I mean, all the planning that we had laid for many years, we had to implement it right away. So we went in there with Mike Withey as our attorney and we went in there with a document saying this is the way we were going to handle dispatch, and this is who is on the dispatch team, this is everyone's role, and this is how we're going to do the dispatch from now on. We went in there and we did that.

What I remember about Silme is his cooking. I have fond memories of watching him cook because he used to like to gather people and cook dinners, a lot for his parents but also for friends, mainly the guys. He'd bring us all together, and we'd watch him cook. He'd cook all these dishes for dinner, but it was such an art for him to cook like that. That's the way he bonded with us a lot. It was through cooking. Other than hanging out, I remember the parties we'd go to and having to pick each other out of the bushes because we drank so much.

Gene was not into the partying and hard-drinking stuff. In fact, he used to criticize us for not being very serious about the work simply because he wasn't a part of the big city, and he didn't like our partying and would always raise it in meetings, like, "You guys aren't very serious about this." They were really two different guys. What brought them together was the passion for the work and the intensity that the work needed in terms of being able to document stuff.

Kalayaan Domingo

Kalayaan is the younger daughter of Silme Domingo and Terri Mast. Her interest in public health led her to a job with the YMCA at Cleveland High School, where she is working on building a community school.

I knew there was something that my mother was sad about, but she didn't talk about it. Nobody really talked directly to me about it. So it was always this thing that was just happening in the background. I wasn't sure what was really going on. It wasn't until my twenties that I probably really understood what was happening. So when I think about my mother during that time, I think about that she was often gone. She was doing something. I missed her a lot, but I also knew that she was sad.

When I was in high school, I did a small project about it, but I really wasn't willing and able to explore more of the emotional side. That was really just about facts and wanting to know what had happened. My own political analysis and consciousness weren't quite developed, and so I couldn't even grasp how huge everything was. And then, when I was in college, I decided to write my senior thesis on it at the urging of a labor studies professor who was familiar with the case, my father and the ILWU [International Longshoremen's and Warehousemen's Union]. She pushed me to explore some of the issues behind it, and so I did a lot of interviews with people, and I was able to start to explore my own emotions around it.

There were people who had expressed a lot of sadness and regret. They were very hesitant to talk to me because it opened up their own sadness. It was very hard for them to talk to me about my own father. A lot of them explained that they weren't ready to and they were just beginning to explore the grief that was behind everything.

My family still doesn't really tell me about my father. They talk about the politics. They talk about the cases. They talk about the character. But they don't tell me stories about my father. There aren't those kinds of candid moments that I'm looking for. I'll hear it as people are in a conversation together, but nobody tells me directly. It's hard for me to ask for that because as I was growing up, I had held my grief in. I feel like that was also something that I was told to do, whether I was told directly or indirectly, to be strong. This is part of a greater movement. I knew that. I knew that it wasn't about one's individual sadness. I never felt like it was okay to cry about it. And if I did, it wasn't okay in public. I also knew that there

were a lot of people who had a lot of sadness around me, so I didn't want to add to that.

I've never had a father. I think that makes it hard for me to grow attached to people because you're always afraid they're going to leave. It's not because it's this imaginary thing. I have a son now, and I imagine what would happen if his dad never came back. I was just a baby, and I didn't have words to tell anybody. And so I don't know how that impacts you. I know that it's something that lives inside me, that feeling. It's not even words that I can explain. It's this ache that's just there that doesn't go away, that's always missing, and I think because I was so young, it's like every experience is colored. When I went to school for the first time, my father wasn't there. When I graduated from college, when I had my son, when I—one day if I get married—it will always be these are all the things that I didn't have. I can't think of something that I did have.

I want to share with my son some of the things that I was missing. I don't think it's as important to know about all the political details. I want him to also have the ability to provide certain analysis around what had happened and how that shapes his life. I want him to know a person. I want him to be able to think about stories. And I hope that our family is able to open up to him. It's been enough time. Maybe they can actually tell him who his grandfather was. He doesn't have grandfathers on either side, so it's a loss for him.

People have told me that I have more of his outgoing personality and that he was kind of wild and liked to party, and I definitely can do that, too. There are times when people have compared me a lot to my dad. Hearing that is actually really nice.

Ligaya Domingo

The elder daughter of Silme Domingo and Terri Mast, Ligaya was three years old when her father was killed. She is now an organizer at SEIU Healthcare 1199NW and aspires to be a professor of Asian American studies.

Even as a kid, I was mimicking what I was seeing. I would conduct meetings with my friends and my sibling and my cousins. We were brought around wherever our parents were going. I remember being in the ILWU Local 37 union hall with them and being there when dispatches were going on, when there were members coming and going. I enjoyed being around all the people. We were taught to call everybody "auntie" and "uncle." I was probably ten or something when I finally realized these people weren't really my family, but I always thought that they were. They were as close to us as our real family was.

It's hard to know what real memories I have of my father because sometimes it's photographs that I've seen and people telling me stories, but I remember going places with him in the International District. I remember going to the Seattle Center with him. I remember going with him to McDonald's when my sister was born. I wasn't allowed to go there, so he took me there, and we had a sundae. I remember my mom being really pissed off that he had taken me somewhere like that. I remember him being very fun-loving.

The night they were shot, I remember feeling just stunned. I didn't know what to think or what was going on. I remember feeling very confused. And then after that, I remember the funeral to some extent. I remember being with my grandparents and just watching like an on-looker, as though I was floating. Again, very confused, not knowing what was really going on. I remember in elementary school, when it was in the news. Kids would come to school and say that they had seen my family on TV.

Right after the case was settled, my grandpa died. It brought up all the emotion from all those years prior to then. The people around me, they were very non-emotional about the whole thing. I think they taught us as kids not to be. They taught us to have a political analysis of the whole thing. But as kids, you have to grieve in order to move on. I didn't want my mom to feel like it was her fault that it was hard for me. She worked so hard as a parent. I felt like I had to pretend like it was okay to some degree to protect her. When I was in high school, she tried to help me the best that she could. It wasn't until I was out of the house and more of an adult that I could sort of take care of it for myself without her being part of the process.

After my first year of college, I went to the AFL-CIO three-day Organizing Institute and started getting trained to be a union organizer at eighteen years old. Through that process, I started understanding my life and experiences more and more, and understanding what my parents' lives were about and what their work

was about. I was just really instilled with this idea about needing to do work that changed the world.

There were several ILWU organizers who were leading the three-day training who worked with my mom and knew that I was her daughter, my dad's daughter, and were themselves quite moved by me being there. Throughout my organizing career, those people have taken me under their wing and have helped to train me and are part of the extended family. Even the union that I work for now, a lot of the people that work there are people that I've known my whole life. Working in the labor movement in a lot of ways is like home to me because I'm with people who understand me on this whole other level because they know my history. In other parts of my life, I've struggled with that issue, of not knowing how to talk to people about it and sometimes just never telling people about it, which is sort of a weird thing, too. How do you tell someone about that part of your life?

I don't think about my father on my own very often. My son brings him up now. I've talked to him about guns as something that can hurt people. And that's all I've told him about that. He knew about my dad being gone, and he's gone to the cemetery with me every year. And then with the thirtieth anniversary, I brought him to both of the events. I explained a little bit more to him, that Lolo, he's not alive anymore. And so of course he asked, "What happened to him?" I told him that some men had hurt him and that he wasn't here anymore. And then, some time recently, he said, "Lolo's gone because someone shot him, Mommy." I have no idea how he knew. When he gets a little older, I will explain to him the work that his grandpa was doing and tell him about what an important man he was, but share with him that it's really sad that he's gone.

Lynn Domingo

The youngest sister of Silme Domingo, Lynn is co-director of the Legacy of Equality, Leadership and Organizing (LELO), a workers' rights organization in Seattle, where she directs a program for low-income families. She has held the post for the past five years.

I was at the University of Washington and there was a summer when I said, "I want to go to Alaska." I wanted to see what my brothers and my father were talking about, and so that was the first year that I joined them. My father paid Tony Baruso and the dispatcher to get me to Alaska. There was a facade of just hanging out at the union hall and signing your papers and just waiting for your name to be called.

It was a whole process that we went through, but we knew essentially that if you paid money, you were employed. I made, like, $2,400 coming home after six weeks, so that was good money for a college student and for seasonal workers. I was dispatched to Egegik.

Alaska was really a horrible, horrible place to work. There was no control at the canneries. There was gang rape. There was so much gambling. Booze was given out to help socialize everyone. It just really ended up being not a humane place. I worked on quality control. It was the canning line. After coming out of the Iron Chink and coming down the conveyor belt, the fish are in the cans. There's the skin that comes out, or bone, and we clean off the sides of the cans. And then the can top slaps right on top of it. So we were there, constantly hearing the slapping of lids on the cans. We would have to dress in cold, yellow water gear and gloves and just make sure all the fish were in line and going up this conveyor, this other piece of machinery, down into the cooker.

We documented the living conditions of the workers, living in bunkhouses where walls were paper-thin. These were old army barracks. I believe they were built as temporaries as they had communal showers and bathrooms. We had to clean up our own areas, while in the other areas, they had people coming in and cleaning them. We had just the worst toilets, the worst showers. It was sometimes worth sleeping in fish guts and old salmon smell and not have to take a shower because it was just as gross in there.

There was also segregation for the women. Emma Catague

and I were roommates. We stayed in those icky bunkhouses, the ones with thin walls. The white women actually had brand new bunkhouses, and we would still work together, but we were segregated. Terri worked in the egg house, and there were other women. They stayed in our bunkhouse, but they chose to do that. It was really set up to have the two different workforces and treatments. We had a lot of fun, but it was a lot of hard work in terms of malnutrition. If you don't have the proper food to work twelve-, eighteen-hour days of three weeks of hard work, you're going to get sick. The women there were also supposed to be playmates, so it wasn't just that they were a real valuable workforce. They were there for other options.

I remember going into the union hall that next day after the murders. There was an organized march down King Street. I didn't go to that march, but I was at the union hall. We were delivered bulletproof vests to wear to work. We were having our windows changed to bulletproof windows. That was a part of the action of going back to work and seizing the union. We were inaugurated and sworn in as officers of the union at that point. I was the secretary-treasurer.

Silme loved velvet suede pants with platforms. He loved current fashion. I would wear his clothes, and his friends would say, "Oh, I saw your sister wearing that shirt," and he would be so mad at me! Gene was satisfied with just a pair of jeans and jean jacket and a T-shirt or whatever. He was just pretty laidback. Even the distinction in their cars—Silme drove a Monte Carlo and Gene drove this little Toyota Corolla that was really gunned out. But they were very similar in terms of their thinking. They were really into reading, and they were very intelligent.

Silme liked working with youth. He liked networking and capacity-building. Gene was quiet, into his writing, mild-mannered. They were very different, but the combination was dynamic. Gene worked on the farm. Silme had it made. He wasn't forced to work like Gene was forced to work. Gene lived among farmworkers every single day of his life and went to school with them and grew up with them. Silme grew up in the inner city. Having that access really created a good movement after their deaths.

I think about Silme all the time, every day, maybe three or four times a day. It's bad because I'm obsessed with it. I asked my husband if I should go see Jimmy Ramil and Ben Guloy. He said it wouldn't do any good. They're going to be there, life in prison with no parole. He said that what I'm doing right now, the community organizing, still being in touch with my community, those are the things that Silme taught me to do because he was my mentor.

There was just so much anger. And mentally, there was just so much anguish. Having a really good family helped. And having a lawyer, a legal team that would pull this together to dialogue, point by point by point, was really important. I left Seattle probably in 1985 and went to California. When I was down there, I realized that I would need to come back and play a role. Otherwise, I would regret it. I needed to be strong. That was my training from the KDP [Union of Democratic Filipinos] collective. So without that collective, I think I would have just broken down. I did go through a lot of binges, but because of that strength, I couldn't really fall so far back.

I believed that I had to go and do something as a young adult outside of my political work, so I disavowed my political work for many years. I thought, "Young adults my age are doing work in an airline or in a store." I wanted to actually go and be a lawyer, but that fell through. I spread my wings and enjoyed traveling, came back in '97, seeing the WTO [World Trade Organization protests] and going, "Okay, I'm restored, and now I'm ready to go back." But that was the period of grieving. It was very, very difficult.

Angel Doniego

Angel was born in the Philippines and came to the United States in 1950, at age ten. He was a founding member of the Union of Democratic Filipinos (KDP), Seattle chapter. He was active in the 1972 Kingdome groundbreaking protest and the march to the Department of Housing and Urban Development to demand funds for developing low-income housing in the International District.

I was pretty much on my own at the age of twelve. I was street-broken, surviving on the street. I went to Vietnam and came back wounded. At the same time, I was involved in something else. And then, I was sent to the Fort Leavenworth military prison, facing a two-and-a-half-year sentence with five of my friends. It was there that I was in contact with ex–Black Panther Party members, the earlier development of the black Islam movement. So I started reading books on Malcolm X. That's when my eyes opened. When I got out of prison, I started to go to Seattle Central Community College. That's when I was introduced to the Oriental Student Union and began to get involved with the Asian movement in '71 and '72.

The Asian movement was up and down the West Coast. It was national. We were all a part of it because there was this sense of our identity as Asians. There was the African American movement—"We're black and we're proud." The Chicanos had theirs. And we were part of this Third World Coalition. My first encounter with the Asian groups was around the domed stadium. At that time, a lot of the younger activists—the Sugiyama brothers, Silme, Peter Bacho, Norris Bacho, Nemesio Domingo, Bob Santos, Frankie Irigon—that's when I began to meet these folks, these activists that I heard so much about. Wow, this is who I wanted to

meet. It was very powerful. For me, it was like an adrenaline rush.

During this period, I met Dale Borgeson. He was passing out a newspaper about martial law in the Philippines and trying to establish a KDP chapter here. I was the first recruited. We also recruited Nora Rebusit. After we began the Seattle chapter, we tried to have a plan to expand. We started to ID certain folks that we needed, that would help us develop this chapter. The priority was Silme.

I worked at Wards Cove for two seasons—'78, '79. We landed in Anchorage and we took a small plane, a four-seater, and then we landed in about one hundred yards of nothing but dirt and pebbles. It was right at the edge of where the ship came in to load and unload. They said, "Okay, this is where the bunkhouse will be." And then there was another bunkhouse, then another bunkhouse. Here we were in the bunkhouse, and it was nothing compared to the whites', where they were living.

When I went to eat, I noticed there were only Filipinos. When I came in before, there were whites and women. What the heck? And then the food that we were getting was, like, "How come this is it? This is all we get for our breakfast?" But the answer from some of the Filipinos was, like, "That's our culture. We wanted salmon instead of that." Yeah, but that's not right. Just to be content with this kind of food while the whites were getting top-of-the-line food.

I was kind of lucky. Although I did spend a little time in the warehouse, I just couldn't do it. It was too cold. So when the assistant foreman's father found out I was a cook, he transferred me to the kitchen. It was my first contact with other Filipinos and to actually see the work and the segregation, the corruption that they talked about in terms of favoritism.

When we started getting active in the KDP here locally, boy, we were drawing attention. My mom was getting calls almost every other day, "You better tell your son to stop that. Tell your son, 'You'll never see your family again.'" So my mom used to cry a lot. I would tell Silme, "I'm scared, man." "What for? Be a man." "I am a man!"

Before the murders, I was seeking another career as a disc jockey, and I was offered a job at a country-and-western station. I was going to take that. That day when I went to resign is the day when the murders happened. I went in to talk to Silme, probably right after lunch, around one or two. I said, "You know, bro', I'm going to be resigning because I've been offered a job in Arizona." And he said, "What? How come you're not sticking around? Screw this thing." "Oh, man, I can't."

Then I went home to prepare. And my stepfather said, "Silme got shot!" I said, "What? What are you talking about?" I just caught a glimpse of the tail end of the news. So I changed my clothes, and I went directly to Harborview. Alonzo and I got there at the same time. When we went to view the body, it was, like, wow. Even up to today, I still could see the tears. I felt a lot of guilt when Silme was murdered. I helped recruit him into the KDP, and I felt like when I was leaving, I was leaving something behind. I said to myself, "I can't leave." So I stayed.

One of the things that we went through after the murders was the rumors from the Tulisan. Some of the rumors I was hearing was that this ain't done. Some more people are coming down. I said, "Bullshit." At that time, we were being trained as a group. So training with weapons, it kind of brought back this, "I'm an ex-military and I'm ready." Some of the other comrades, this was the first time they ever held a weapon. To go down to the union every day with a bulletproof vest and at the same time participating and making sure that even the windows, "No, this has to be changed." For security, we worked in teams and never traveled by ourselves.

I had a couple of guns. I wanted revenge. But of course there was the KDP that helped me balance it. In '84, I heard there was a contract out on me, so I was moving from place to place. Actually, I was staying in the same apartment where Terri was staying, to be close to her. I just felt that I had a role to play here because of my military experience and my experience as a gangbanger when I was young, living on the streets. I thought that I was more experienced in dealing with some of this shit than they were.

Silme was like a brother to me. He was crazy. He had a lot of humor. He had a big heart. I've never seen anybody like that, with so much energy, a lot of compassion toward his work, toward the Asian community. I had never seen anybody like that, except when I was in prison. But he was the first one that I ever felt that real desire, compassion, to really move this shit forward, to get some justice, to actually do this movement that we were talking about, this anti–martial law. I would say, "Damn, don't you ever stop?" He would say, "What for?"

Dick Farinas

In 1969, Dick Farinas became the first Filipino American hired by the Equal Employment Opportunity Commission (EEOC) as an investigator. He helped establish the Seattle office and handled many cases, including the complaints against the Alaska canneries. He retired from the EEOC in 1991.

In those days, from the '50s when I came in, up to the '70s and even as far as '80, minorities had a hard time to get into any halfway decent jobs, except dishwashing, gardening, washing windows, washing cars... Those were the only jobs we could get into regardless of whether you had four or five degrees from any university. They didn't really recognize the ability or the worth of any minority worker.

I majored in marketing, business administration, and minored in political science. After graduating in 1954, I applied for jobs everywhere. I applied for a job at the National Bank of Commerce. We were sent downtown to their office, and it was twenty-four of us selected by the University of Washington (UW) to work there, and we were supposed to be interviewed—all twenty-four of us—because they had already slotted twenty-four positions. Four o'clock in the afternoon, closing time. I was the only one still sitting in my chair waiting to be interviewed and they were preparing to get out. I said, "Have you any time to interview me?" He said, "What's your name?" And I said, "Ricardo Farinas, Dick Farinas." "We don't have the paperwork here." "You don't have—" So I looked at the wastebasket, and my application was there. I said, "Oh, that's it. I won't be able to get a job here. And I will never be able to get a job here in the U.S. as far as knowing the law and their attitude toward me or any minority. I won't have any chance."

I was able to get on board in 1969 with the Equal Employment Opportunity Commission. I was the first Filipino hired by EEOC as an investigator. So they sent me to San Francisco. We took classes at the University of San Francisco strictly on civil rights law. After six months, they said, "You go back to Seattle. You guys open up an office." So we opened up this office here. I opened up at the Hogue Building. That was the middle of 1970. Since then, after my training in San Francisco, I started investigating. I went all over the U.S.

During my school days at the UW, a lot of us students there had been recruited by the late Gene Navarro. He said, "You schoolboys come down and I'll try to find room for you to go to Alaska for your school finances." I said, "Sure, thank you." So they asked for an allotment from the different canneries. They said, "Take four or five schoolboys. Let's help our boys go up to Alaska." I worked in the canneries first before I became an investigator for the federal government.

I went to Waterfall Cannery, the first cannery where I worked. I went there in 1951 and '52. Then I skipped one year. After that, I went to Sunny Point Cannery at Ketchikan. I did two seasons at Sunny Point and then one at

Columbia Wards Fisheries at Alitak, Alaska, Kodiak Island. I was a jitney driver. I wasn't lifting nothing, just driving the jitney with a loaded cart behind; I was pulling this cart. That was my job.

I was complaining against the cannery management then. They want us to do this, clean this up, clean that up. I said, "Let's see that in the union agreement with the canneries, whether it involves this kind of work." The old folks were getting mad at me. "Don't rock the boat! Don't rock the boat!" So I just kept quiet. I said, "I'm not going to come here anyhow. Later on, I might be able to find a job."

My wife's father was the cannery foreman at Wards Cove cannery in Ketchikan, and some of his crew were some of his grandsons, sons, and relatives, etc. Her nephews were complaining then. They said, "Why do we have to do this? Why do we have to do that? If they want us to do nonunion work, they should compensate us for doing these things." I was already with EEOC in 1970. In 1972, her nephew was working at Wards Cove. He was the one complaining against this cannery. "Don't embarrass me. I'm your grandfather." "Yes, Grandpa, but we're not supposed to be doing this."

I heard about this complaint, so I said, "Let's talk about it." I approached Winn Brindle at that time, the owner of the Wards Cove cannery, and I said, "What seems to be the problem here?" "We don't have any problem." "Winn, it seems to me that there's some exploitation going on here on your part of your minority employees." He said, "What would that be?" "Well, I heard this rumor that you're making these people work, nonunion work." And he said, "I don't know." So they resolved that as a grandfather and grandson.

But then, during that summer of 1972, Kevin Ebat went to one of these New England Fish Company canneries, and he saw the difference between the living conditions of the Caucasian employees and the Filipinos or other minority employees in terms of the condition of housing, bedding in all the facilities, washing machines, bathroom. Everything was so different. I knew that because I experienced it personally myself. Nothing had changed. So I fashioned a commissioner's charge, United States Equal Opportunity Commission versus the canneries in Alaska.

So now I investigated. I was sent there by EEOC. "Well, you are expert in this," they said. "You go." So I went all over Alaska from 1972 to 1978. And I think I went there the last time in 1980 as part of a compliance review of the canneries as far as the implementation of the adjustments they made.

Silme and Michael Woo helped me document everything that was going on in Uganik Bay. I said, "Before you go there, bring a camera. Do not show it. Take pictures of the bedrooms, anything that you can. And I want a copy." So that really made my investigation strong. My evidence was there, and I sent it to Washington, D.C. They notified the whole canning industry. They said, "Here's what's going on. Here is the evidence that we have gathered there." We asked them whether they wanted to conciliate the case or deny it, in which case, "We'll see you in Supreme Court." They said, "No, okay. We agree." I wasn't the conciliator then. There was another bunch of lawyers who were assigned for that. I did the investigation.

So I went there doing compliance review of my investigations, whether they are implementing or trying to abide by the law or not, where they were. I said, "Hey, you have to im-

prove on the washing machines. Sixty Filipinos using one washing machine for their clothes. No, you have to make it on par with the white people." They said, "Oh, my God! That's a lot of expenses." I said, "Well, let's trade places. You be the Filipino and I am the white person, and I give you one of these washing machines to use. How would you feel?" They said, "Okay, fine." They did make some improvements, but the cannery owners are so slick.

Filipinos were doing the egg-processing work in all the canneries. To minimize expenses, they stopped processing the salmon eggs in Alaska. They sold the salmon whole. They were shipping them to Japan, and the Japanese were the ones pulling the eggs in Japan. So now they were shipping less and less people to Alaska to work in the canneries because the jobs weren't there anymore.

I'm a Wapato boy. I babysat Gene. Felix Viernes is Gene's father. Felix Viernes and my dad were partners in farming, and so when Gene was a little boy, they used to come to our house in Wapato and I used to take care of him when my dad and his father worked on the farm. I just watched him and changed diapers. I knew the whole family. We saw each other every day there. I was going to school then at the UW, but during the summertime, I went back and helped them on the farm.

I knew Silme. We were very close. We talked all the time. We knew the Domingos through the community. And my children and Silme and Gene were close because they all went to school together at the UW.

John Foz

Born and raised in San Francisco, California, John attended San Francisco State University. He came to Seattle to work with the ILWU Local 37 reform movement. He worked for two seasons in Alaska. John was a contributor to the Alaskero News, *doing illustrations, headlines and layout. He is currently secretary of the Puget Sound Region of the Inlandboatmen's Union of the Pacific and serves on the board of International Community Health Services in Seattle.*

I was a member of the Union of Democratic Filipinos in the Bay Area. There were people that had come up to help with the reform movement. It turned out that they needed more people. I was in a situation where I could use the work, and so I came up in May of 1979 and got involved. In order to impact the reform work, the Rank-and-File Committee needed people to get jobs in Alaska in what was identified as key canneries, so I needed to get dispatched and I needed to become a member of the union. They wanted to get me up to the Wards Cove Ketchikan cannery, but as a new person with no seniority or experience, I had no chance. The way I finally got up was that Nemesio Domingo, Sr. was an officer and he put in a good word that I was the grandnephew of Vincent Foz, a retired foreman of Wards Cove Excursion Inlet cannery near Juneau. It was from that connection that, many dispatches later, I was inevitably sent up to Alitak on Kodiak Island, a Columbia Wards Fisheries plant.

I worked in a wet job, in the fish house. I worked on the butcher machine, on the Iron Chink, and also in a new freezer operation. The Iron Chink was at the 1909 Alaska-Yukon-Pacific Exposition. It was a machine that beheaded, eviscerated, and split open the salmon carcasses in preparation for slimers, who would take out the fins and the bloodline, etc. The Iron Chink was actually named for the Chinese workers who preceded the mechanization of the fish house. It was a very strange, very racist tribute to the Chinese who preceded the Filipinos into the canneries.

There were *manongs* from California who continued to follow the asparagus, grapes, and into the seasons of working in Alaska. There were also some local old-timers who had been going up for many, many years, some of whom at this point in the late '70s were followed by their sons and daughters.

It was quite interesting working with these old-timers. I had been exposed to old-timers, particularly in my work in San Francisco. I was involved during college in the struggle for the preservation of low-income housing in the International Hotel in San Francisco, but this was different. A lot of these old-timers carried a lot of history in Alaska. They had a lot of information to share with the younger folks about how much of a better life we had as a result of the sacrifices that they've made. It was also interesting, too, because there was also a new wave of Filipino immigrants who were also following the route of the first wave of Filipinos. These were newer immigrants who were still doing agricultural work in cities like Delano and Stockton. And there was also a new influx of college students of varied backgrounds, Anglo and Asian college students from Oregon and Washington. So the workforce was very diverse and changing.

I was acquainted with Gene and Silme through the Union of Democratic Filipinos work, but I didn't know them well. I didn't get to know them that well until I moved up here. You couldn't ask for two more different people. Gene seemed quite serious, quite stoic. He had his playful moments, but by and large, he was a very serious personality, somewhat brooding, whereas Silme was just totally gregarious and always joking and joshing.

But the one constant between the two of them was that they were very dedicated to the cause of reforming the union. They shared that very strongly together.

Some people have stated, "What would these murders signify?" The larger picture was, we were up against some pretty big international forces as it turned out. The Marcos dictatorship had long tendrils into the Filipino American community. That is one lesson for people that are going up against forces like that, to not underestimate what we're up against, that there are some real powerful forces that you run up against internationally, that they're going to come back at you.

If these murders and the reform of the union had not happened, it's hard to say where the cannery workers union would be. It's hard to say where both the ILWU and the IBU [Inlandboatmen's Union] would be, to be honest, because it enlivened a whole international view of the labor movement in a way that it took their blood to do that. We could say their lives were for the sake of trade unions around the world.

I can still hear their voices and their laughter. Thirty years hasn't tarnished that much my memory of them. I guess I would be their *manong* now. I could just really see us talking about what's going on politically now, both in the labor movement and in the Philippines. I'm sure we'd have some pretty interesting conversations. They had very interesting perspectives on people in the community and political events. There was no lack of interesting conversation around those guys about things that were going on. Never a dull moment, so to speak.

It seemed to be such a natural thing back in the 1960s and '70s for so many people to get involved. The Vietnam War was going on, the Marcos dictatorship, rampant abuses. People were taking to the streets. It was easier to organize because people were ready, willing, available. It was the thing to do. It's a lot tougher when there's more of a political lull. I think there is a need, from one generation of organizers to another, to instill among people some very basic organizing skills to make sure that people know why they're doing what they're doing. And hold their hand as far as you can take them until they can run with whatever is going on.

Although it's encouraging to see some of the efforts going on among the younger generation, it's very different. People are way more tech-savvy, maybe a little bit more tech-dependent as opposed to organizing-dependent. But people are tapped in. If anything, they realize more than ever that information is power. What was the quote I read somewhere? I think it was a quote from Jefferson, "Information is the currency of democracy." That struck me as an interesting statement.

As for the cannery workers union, it's totally different now. The industry is totally different. A lot of economic and political forces have shaped where it is now. It's totally different than in years past. What the future holds, who knows? There are still, I believe, opportunities, especially with the new workforce, which is now totally an immigrant workforce from overseas. There are new challenges to organize that workforce, and the things that they face, like some of the big trawler ships, etc. So those are some new challenges. But I think people have been pretty creative about trying to address that over the decades. People probably never thought that Local 37 was organizable, you know, back in the day. So I hold out a lot of hope, hold on to the shred of hope that organizing is possible, that organizers will come out of adversity.

Rich Gurtiza

Rich has served as director of Region 37 of the Inlandboatmen's Union of the Pacific since 1993. A Wapato native, he moved to Seattle in 1976. He attended Central Washington College with Gene Viernes, majoring in political science. He served as president of Filipino American Political Action Group of Washington from 2003 to 2011.

I was born in Yakima, and my folks lived in the lower valley. They were farmers. We had approximately 160 acres in the rural west Wapato area. Wapato actually is a small farming community. I think the population is about 3,800 people. It's spread out in rural areas. At that time, during the '70s and even during the '60s, the employers of the Alaska seafood industry did a lot of recruiting down in this area, Wapato, and also in the San Joaquin Valley in Stockton and Delano, California. There were a lot of prospective cannery workers there because the employer knew that they could do the grueling work that was necessary in the industry.

A lot of the younger men took them up on their offer of working the summers in the Alaska seafood industry. And so it was a traditional thing with the younger generation working in Alaska. In fact, our forefathers actually got started working in the Alaska seafood industry. And then the next generation graduated up. I'm a second-generation Filipino American. It was pretty much a rite of passage in terms of going to work in the canneries.

I have three other brothers, and we all did a duty up there at one time or another. I got dispatched to Wards Cove in Ketchikan. That was the original Wards Cove cannery. And then I worked up in Bumblebee, which is in Bristol Bay, a short season for the sockeye run. I worked at another place, a floating processor, Icicle Seafoods, down in the bay as well. So I spent approximately five seasons working in the industry.

When I first went up to Alaska in 1977, they wanted me to be a slimer. The slimer is when the fish comes out of the butcher machine, it comes out with part of the membrane still intact—it's also known as the bloodline that runs down the back spine of the salmon. You have to clean that out along with any other extra things that the butcher machine doesn't take off. You clean the fish off, you have a knife, and hundreds of fish are coming off the belt, and you have to do it very quickly. You're standing there with water dripping down. You're trying to clean the membrane and the entire fish as fast as possible because it goes next onto the canning line.

So when I first got there, I was a greenhorn, and the foreman wanted to put me on this line of twenty-five men, standing where all this fish were coming through, hundreds at a time, coming to you. I refused to do that job. I knew, being twenty years old, I couldn't stand for eighteen hours a day and really didn't want to try. So I told the foreman, "Give me the hardest job. Give me a job that nobody wants." And so he put me out on unloading the boats, which was a hard job because you unloaded fish. You had to push the fish out of the boat and into this elevator, which took the fish into the plant. Essentially, you had to touch every fish because it was the only way to unload it. It was very labor intensive and very difficult. You had hip boots on and you were sometimes up to your neck in fish, and nobody wanted to do it. But I thought it was a good job since I was outside and moving all the time. That was my first job.

The work itself didn't faze me because I was brought up with a positive work ethic. I was baling hay when I was ten years old, one hundred–pound bales of hay. So that kind of work was actually good for me because I didn't have to be in one hundred–degree heat in the summertime in Wapato.

At the time, I wasn't necessarily involved in the movement or in the union. Their deaths affected me on a more personal level. To this day, I think Gene was trying to protect me from all that. He was doing union work and he was telling me about some threats that he was getting being a dispatcher. It wasn't until after the murders that I realized how bad it was and what he was up against. I didn't ask, and he never really shared that with me. I'd say, "Let's go to this place to have a drink or something," and he says one time, "Well, I can't go there because there are some gangsters who hang out there." Now I know why he didn't want to go to those places.

I got involved after the murders, and it wasn't just me. It was many people. That's when I felt the people who were organizing understood what it meant and decided to step forward. As Gene and Silme put themselves out there, I think the mentality was that they couldn't get everybody. If everybody put out an effort to try to change the union, they'd have too many targets.

I have been organizing for at least twenty years. I continue to do the work because I feel an obligation, not only to Gene and to Silme, but to the people who came before and the people who are continuing to come, to negotiate the best contract and conditions I can for them. I could see myself doing something else, but I don't necessarily know how I could move on without taking the union experience out with me.

Silme and Gene lived life to the fullest. They never looked back and they had one thing in common. They always gave. I hate to use the old cliché, but they'd give you the shirt off their back. Both of them were the same way. I remember a time when I didn't know Silme all that well. He came to the house one time and I remember I had a date and no car. Silme had that really nice Monte Carlo car and I had this broken-down Volkswagen bus. And Silme says, "Take the car. Take my car." I go, "What?" He goes, "Yeah, take the car and go out on your date." And so I did. I really wanted to impress her, and I couldn't believe that he would do that for me, but that's the way he was.

Silme was a heck of a cook. We had this party for a crew that came back from Kodiak and he was cooking at the house where Gene and I lived, and we watched him do his thing. Silme had no problem sharing cooking techniques. He says, "Well, you gotta put sugar in this." He tells me how and everything. To this day, I still use that stuff and realize that Silme was the one who taught me how to do that.

I could go on and on about Gene, growing up in a small town and the things that he did. But I will just say that he came from a very large family. Growing up in the area, we were pretty poor. A lot of us were, and especially his family. They didn't have much, but Gene always gave. He never had anything, even when we were living together. He'd put all his resources to his younger brothers and sisters, put Stan through college and did everything basically for them. Everything he just gave to everybody else. So those are the things that I admire, the character that they had and the value they put on friendship and what they would do for others and not take back for themselves. Those are the values that I just try to emulate.

They were an odd couple, Gene and Silme. Gene was more of a country guy, and he didn't really care what he looked like. He'd wear this old Levi's jacket. He'd wear jeans—his jeans all had holes in them. He was always in a T-shirt; he was always really casual all the time. And Silme would have slacks. He'd have platform shoes, and he'd be very dressed. He'd be really tidy. Gene's hair, it seemed he never combed it or nothing. He'd get up and shower and just throw on his hat and go. But Silme was always perfectly manicured and drove a nice car. He got inside the car, he smelled really nice. Gene, he drove around in whatever he could. As far as their character, values, and personalities, they were basically on the same page.

John Hatten

*Son of union, civil rights, and criminal law at-
torney C. T. "Barry" Hatten, John grew up among
U.S. Communist Party activists. He has worked
as an emergency medical technician, taught elementary school, cofounded and taught at an independent high school, and, since 2000, has owned a
computer and networking repair business, Kulshan
Computer Service. He lives in Bellingham, Washington with his wife and two daughters.*

My dad was a left-wing attorney. When things
were tough being an attorney, he did longshor-
ing. And so he was in this community, the
International District-Chinatown. He had become Local 37's attorney a long time ago and
just did all kinds of legal work for them. He
was never rich. He was just one of these people
that liked to do good.

One time, I walked into his office down
on King Street. He said, "Hey, John. You need
a watch?" I said, "No. Why?" "Because I got
some watches." He rolled up his sleeve, and I
guess he decided to start collecting them on
his arm from clients that couldn't afford to pay
and he'd take their watches.

It was 1972 when I first went up to Alaska.
I was seventeen, and you had to be eighteen to
get a job up there. But my dad talked to who-
ever he talked to and was able to get me a job.
All I had to do was say I was eighteen. And so
I started working in Peter Pan Seafoods, Hawk
Inlet, up on Admiralty Island. I was making
great wages. Minimum wage was about sixty
cents and I was making a buck ninety, so I
thought I was pretty hot. You didn't have any
way to spend your money, and so whatever you
made, you took a good hunk of change home
at the end of the summer.

That first year, I did a whole bunch of
things. It seemed like they moved me wherever
they wanted me. At one point, I was working
in the egg room, where the fish had their heads
chopped off and then you stuck your fingers
in and pulled out the egg sacks. The cleaner

you could pull those egg sacks out, the happier
the Japanese, who were buying them, would
be. I did that. I did some forklift driving for
a while.

Probably the most memorable experience
of Hawk Inlet was that there was a fire in the
Native village, just down the boardwalk. It was
just horrifying, the poverty that was there. But
here, we were mostly Filipino, and then me,
the token white guy. And just seeing the poverty of the Native people who were trying to
make a buck working there. They had expenses
they had to pay for. They had to pay for their
houses, they had to pay for their food, everything. Whereas when we came in, it was all
taken care of. That was a pretty striking thing
for a seventeen-year-old kid. Not that I hadn't
seen poverty before, but just to see that right
up against my face.

I worked a total of six seasons at various
canneries. Then I came back, and I think it was
maybe in that year or maybe a year or two later
when Gene called me up and said, "Hey, we've
got this reform movement in the union, and
we thought we would talk to you about it." I
had been involved in antiwar stuff in Vietnam,
and I wanted to change the world, make it a
better place, and they seemed like similar, like-
minded people. Didn't really know anything
about the union except that was the place we
paid our dues and that was where we got dispatched. I knew my dad was an attorney for
the union, but whatever. So I started meeting.

I just remember going there to meet and
just thinking, wow, here's a bunch of young
people that are wanting to reform the union,
because they told me stories that I didn't know,
about corruption, bribery, and stuff like that.
I said, "That's not right. Of course, I want to
change that." I was in a unique position to run
because so many people knew and liked my
dad. There was a position open for trustee of
the union. I didn't really know that much, although I had been raised with political awareness. I ran, and maybe to everybody's surprise,

I won. Maybe I was unopposed, I don't know, but I became a trustee of Local 37.

Back before the Rank-and-File Committee was something that the major, mainstream union even knew about, I was taking minutes or notes. Tony Baruso saw me writing. I'm a horrible speller, and I remember him teasing me about my spelling. I just remember being struck by that later. It was kind of like a moment of rapport or something, even though he was teasing me about my spelling.

Later on, Tony was brought up on charges and I testified against him. It was some malfeasance. It was corruption or something. It wasn't murder. I don't think my testimony was particularly damning, but I was there to say what I had seen in the union. I just remember carrying that juxtaposition of him correcting my spelling, which I still remember to this day because I can't spell.

I remember Silme as this really charismatic, amazing, go-getter kind of personality. He was just a really nice guy. Gene I remember as being quieter, just sharp as a tack. If there was something, he was on it. They were two of the brightest folks around. That was the thing that was so poignant about it all. To take two of the brightest minds in our community and then to have them be lost. It was just really hard.

The major achievement of the reform movement was shedding daylight on a system that was really behind closed doors. The reason it was successful was that so many people had had experience paying Gene Navarro or basically knowing that there was corruption going on, not getting the best job because somebody else did it. So when some young people said, "There's a better way to do this," it really resonated. That's the thing that we need to think about today. What is the message that we have that's going to resonate with people today? It's finding a message that speaks truth. You might be Republican. You might be Democrat. But what is your experience, and are we speaking to it? If we're speaking to your experience, it

works. And that's what was happening then.

There was a young girl from Seattle Pacific College who was at Port Bailey. We were all going to work after dinner because there was overtime. Her glove got caught in the grinder, where they ground the fish to top it off to make it the right weight in these cans. Her hand got chopped off. I was an emergency medical technician at the time. I went into first-aid mode, and then I cried my eyes out for maybe an hour. Just how grievously sad it was that this young girl had lost a hand, and how unfair it was.

As a teenager, as an early-twenties person, as with this young girl, there's a sense of invincibility that is false. It was dangerous work. There were really big machines that if you put your hand in the wrong place, you could get really hurt. It sticks to me so plainly, this young kid who now must be in her fifties. That's one of the things that is really important to me. We're talking about a labor union that made lives a whole lot better for a whole lot of people. I'm really glad the Rank-and-File Committee came along and cleaned up the corruption. The bottom line is it was there before that. What Chris Mensalvas, Sr. and others had started was a foundation of unity among workers.

We had a contract that allowed us grievances. This was a really important thing, and even as a seventeen-year-old, I knew that it was really good that we were in a union. I had a friend later who said he had heard about me going up a couple years in a row. He said, "I got to get me one of those Alaska jobs." He went up. They were packed into one giant bunkhouse just like sardines. They were paid poorly. They were fired on a whim, no transportation paid to and from. It was a horrendous situation. We were in contact, and I found out about it and went to visit him just as he was calling the Department of Labor to shut this place down. Whew! So just being a part of the union, my first experience was, "Yes, this was the right way to be doing it."

Julia Laranang

Julia worked as a staff member for the Alaska Cannery Workers Association and as a writer for the International Examiner *in the 1970s. Since 1993, she has been employed as a management systems analyst at Seattle Center, working on free and low-cost public programs, including cultural festivals and youth-based programs.*

You meet Silme, and he's Mr. Casual, very outgoing. We were instantly friends. I think he was like that with a lot of people. He was very passionate about what he was doing. It was almost like he evangelized for it because he wanted to tell people about it and talk. Silme and I and other people, probably half a dozen times, drove to California and back. And somehow, Silme and I ended up being the people in the middle of the night that would be driving the car, and everyone else was sleeping. So we'd talk about everything from "Was there something beyond the stars?" to "Do you ever want to have kids?"

It was almost infectious when you were around him that you would have a good time. As much as he was a guy with a kind of goofball sense of humor, he was very serious about getting done what he wanted to get done. I believe that if it wasn't for him, a lot of other people might have fallen by the wayside.

The ACWA office became a place where the guys that were involved in the lawsuits or that were working in the canneries in the off-season would come hang out. I got to know a lot of them that way. A lot of them were away from home because they were from other parts of the country. That's how I met Gene, because Gene was from Wapato. I remember he came in with all these pictures of the differences between where the longshoremen, the white guys, got to stay and where the Filipinos and Native Americans and black guys got to stay. He just had pictures of really, really contrasting conditions, and I thought, "This guy!" I don't know at the time if he had meant to file

a lawsuit, but he certainly did the background work that made it possible. I believe that was for the Wards Cove case.

There was a time—it was really funny, because it was about three or four months after I finally married Earl after ten years of being with him—the three of us, Silme, me, and Gene, drove to California and back. They thought, "We must be pretty cool if your husband lets you go to California with us." And I said, "Either that or he knows you guys are no threat." They went, "No! We're macho guys!"

Gene was quiet. I remember having long conversations with him, but only in private. Gene was a lot more focused on the lawsuits, the nuts-and-bolts part of it and the process. Silme was more the getting-the-people-involved kind of person, but I think there was a part of Silme that sometimes got a little tired of being in the limelight.

There was a time before he and Terri became a permanent couple, when she was pregnant with her first child. Very early in the pregnancy, there were people that were actually pressuring him to pressure her to have an abortion. Silme was really struggling with that, not because he wanted Terri to have an abortion, but these people were giving all these logical reasons why this wasn't a good time to do this.

One morning on my way to work, because we had talked the night before, I went to his place and woke him up. I said, "You know what, Silme? You can do whatever you want with your relationship with Terri, but she wants this child. This may be her last chance to have a child. You need to understand that this is her decision, and you need to honor whatever that decision is." And he looked at me and said, "No, it's my decision, too. It's my child, and we're going to have it. And thank you for caring enough."

He wasn't just a guy that was interested in politics. He wanted a family, and he really cared about Terri. I don't think he ever seriously considered not having that child, but he was just struggling with "What do I tell these people?" These other people had nothing to do with it. It was just their decision.

Every once in a while, I think about them. I'll start to think, "What would have happened had they stayed alive?" But I'm kind of a person that believes things happen because they're supposed to. In my mind, they'll be forever young. They'll be forever passionate. I look at what happened to some of the other folks, and most of us are doing pretty good, but a lot of us have lost whatever it is that makes you want to go out and change the world. We've gotten a little more fatalistic. What I remember most about them doesn't have to do with politics or the lawsuits. There are certain people that are just different. I would have trusted either one of those people with my life, and I'm not saying I was exclusive. I'm not saying I was their best friend, but I'm saying that's the kind of people they were.

My kids are grown now, but my boys remember them, from when they were growing up. Silme and Gene taught them how to pitch pennies against the wall for money. They weren't one-dimensional people, and they never forgot that people came first. There are some people that get so zealous about their political cause that they sacrifice people. They didn't do that. And that is a lesson that a lot of us can learn.

They were quite openly Communist, but it wasn't as it was in the '50s, when Joseph McCarthy was running around calling people things. It wasn't people looking to overturn the American government. It was people that wanted to make our society better. They felt that some of the ways things worked were not working. They didn't want to destroy America. They wanted to put a set of principles in place that would make it better.

The Weather Underground at one time contacted us. That scared the heck out of me. I got to work and there was a little piece of paper on the door that said, "Greetings. This is your friendly Weather Underground, and we've left a present for you." And I went, "Uhhh, nooo." I called one of the guys and said, "I'm not doing this." As it turned out, it was just a bunch of newspapers. Then I got a visit from one of the news-radio people. I forgot his name, but he said, "Yeah, I heard you got something from the Weather Underground." I was thinking, "How did he know that?" It was kind of scary.

It's interesting because people are doing way different things now. They're running museums. They're attorneys. I've always felt a little bit of an outsider because by the time I got involved, I was a few years older than some of the other folks. Most of them were college students. I had been done with college by that time. I had two kids, so I had another dynamic. I was a little older, but I think that was an advantage. But it was interesting to observe the various backgrounds of people that came together because they had common caring. People that you almost want to describe as Asian princesses in the sense that they came from a very spoiled—not wealthy—but well-off background. But they cared. They wanted to come and do stuff.

And kids like Gene, who came from a family that works in the fields of Wapato. Then you got some middle-class folks, blue-collar dad that worked his way up. Silme's mom worked in a bank. They had very different growing-up backgrounds, but when they came together, you'd think they'd been together all their lives because they cared about wanting to make things better and they had a specific interest in keeping the Asian community and the International District—which is really the home of it—as our community and not just a tourist attraction.

There was a time when they were building the Kingdome when we wanted to meet with the county executive and he didn't want to meet with us. I remember a lot of people came to help us. That's where I met Sue Mo-

rales and Ramona Bennett from the Puyallup Tribe. We went down there and literally took over the office and walked into his conference room. There was a drawing on the wall that had the Kingdome. And, you know, for a long time, those freeway ramps that were incomplete? Well, the freeway ramp was complete and it went right over the International District. All that was in the drawing was a couple of hotels and restaurants. There was no International District. It was just this freeway ramp going to the Kingdome. I was very sorry that someone got really mad and tore that down. I would have loved to have kept it. People just said, "Oh, no. We can't have this." It really galvanized people to come together and work together—*hum bows*, not hot dogs. So it was a very real threat. It wasn't just imagined.

Terri Mast

Terri is the widow of Silme Domingo. She first began working in Alaska as a cannery cook and became involved with the Alaska Cannery Workers Association, doing legal work, organizing, outreach, and financial administration. As a Rank-and-File Committee activist, she helped reform Local 37 of the ILWU and was elected the union's first woman local officer. Terri has been serving as the national secretary-treasurer of the Inlandboatmen's Union since 1993.

For me, the thing I feel lucky about back then was the relationship I had in meeting some of the older people—Chris Mensalvas, Sr., Barry Hatten, who was the attorney for the union for years, John Caughlan. Being able to sit down and have drinks with them and talk about their histories is really what influenced me and gave me my political insight. Most of those old-timers were part of the Communist Party, and so they had no hesitancy talking about their experiences and what they went through to be political activists. That was exciting and that was what really politicized me.

One of the clearest examples of sexism within the union was one time when I was set to go to Alaska. And then I had a baby. I was supposed to go the next summer. I'm gearing up this whole time, thinking, "I'm going, I'm planning, I'm preparing. I'm going to Alaska." And it was only a month before I was supposed to go when Gene and Silme said to me, "We think maybe you shouldn't go to Alaska anymore." And I said, "Why? I'm prepared. I'm ready. I've done everything. I understand everything. I've applied to two different companies. I've been hired by two companies. Why am I not going?" "Well, you have the baby."

So it was a big struggle about should I or shouldn't I still go and why I should go. It was Silme's baby, too, and so there was a lot of discussion and struggle about it. In the end, I went. We figured out how to take care of the baby while I was gone. We were in a po-

litical organization where we talked about sexism and the effects on women, and so at least they were willing to have discussions about it. Sometimes it was difficult to work with them and to bring out those issues.

I think just having that experience, in the end, when it came time to step up, in some ways it was easier, because I had already been challenged enough that it wasn't that I didn't have the confidence, that they didn't try to give me the confidence. I never felt they tried to hold me back.

After the murders, I didn't really feel I was the person to step up. Having two kids who just lost one parent. Is that really what I should do? That was a real question. And then, just having the real experience to do it. Was I the best person? But in a number of other ways, it made sense. It could have been easier to say, "Let David do it" or "Someone else should do it." But there were a lot of needs on people at the same time. I also got support from everyone. It didn't feel like it was just me doing it. It really was all of us stepping in and working collectively to do it. That's what gave me the strength to do it. And also the relationships that I had had with Silme and Gene and the training that they had given us allowed us to be able to do that.

I hear their voices all the time. I hear them telling me, kind of pushing me to do things, especially things like speaking or sometimes when I'm trying to write something and I get stuck. Sometimes it will just start flowing, and I know it's not necessarily my voice. It's a different voice speaking inside.

The girls were pretty good girls, so that helped. We had our challenges, but I think we have a bond that's different than most parents and children have. I know for Ligaya, she didn't want to create anything else that was going to hurt me. So when other people complain to me about parenting, I'm like, "You're talking to the wrong person. You got two parents, you got a husband." It's not like we were paid a lot either at the union. That was the other challenge. We were really not paid well. That was one of the reasons Emily moved in with me, just financially to help.

Every year, we did a memorial, for at least a good ten, maybe more, years. So the girls definitely grew up living it. And their family is known. People knew what happened to their father almost no matter where they went.

My younger daughter, Kalayaan, was not even a year old. She has the least memory of her father and of the event. So she goes off to college in California, and she called me one day and said, "I was sick, and I went to see the nurse. The nurse came in and said my name perfectly. And so I thought, 'Hmm, this is strange, because she's a white woman, but she said my name perfectly.' She took me back to the room and said, 'You probably don't remember me, but I used to change your diapers.'" She was someone who had lived in Seattle and was part of the Committee for Justice and knew her when she was a child. That would happen to her almost wherever she went.

Ligaya was older and had some of the same experiences with the Committee for Justice and being involved. She also went away for college. And one night, she calls me, saying, "I get it! I get it! I understand now what you do. I understand labor. I understand what you do." She had taken some class and they had sent her out to do some kind of initiative signing or something. She was out talking to people, getting them to sign something, and all of a sudden, everything clicked about what the role of labor and what some of my work was.

She became very interested and tried to understand the labor movement and what we were doing and why we would be involved in the labor movement. She came back here and went to school and then started working for a union, became a union organizer. So she got involved in a different way, but through her own understanding of what it was that her parents were doing.

I like my job. I like being in the labor movement. For me, it's still being part of a movement. I think the labor movement is the only hope for the working class in this country, so I enjoy doing that. It's personally rewarding to me. I think at this point, I also bring something to the table.

Labor is more relevant today than ever. The need for workers to be organized is also very necessary. I think a lot of young workers don't understand that. They don't understand the history of labor, especially now, given the economic crisis that we're in. The lessons that we need to teach those people is that when you're organized into a union, you certainly have more of a voice and have the support of people around you to step up.

The laws are not in our favor. And so it does take some courage and some support for workers to be able to do that. So I think the lesson we learned is exactly that. If people are working together and there's a movement and you support each other, then we can reach those goals. We can fight against whatever big employer it is and be successful. It's not just you. You're not alone.

Chris Mensalvas, Jr.

Son of a famed union organizer and former president of ILWU Local 37, Chris worked for more than three decades in the Alaska canneries. He was a plaintiff in the class action lawsuit against Wards Cove Packing Company. Chris has had a lifelong interest in art, creating graphic illustrations and making intricate wood carvings. He has lived for many years in Mexico, where he finds inspiration for his work in the abundant natural landscape around him.

———————————

My mother died before I was a year old. And then my father had a hard time taking care of us, so he sent my sister and me to the Philippines. My dad's plan was to come over later and live there permanently. But he was having problems with the government here, so each year, he would say, "I'll be coming over," but it just kept extending, extending. My sister and I, we were there about eight years until he finally told us, "You can come back now." Then we went to Hawaii. My dad was living in Hawaii then.

As long as I've known my dad, he was always involved in union work, even in Hawaii. And the reason why he didn't go to the Philippines, what I heard, is that he was told by some of his labor contacts in the Philippines that he would be assassinated as soon as he got there. So he stayed in Hawaii and called us back. It was the McCarthy era. He was considered a Communist. He had a lot of meetings at home and did a lot of fund-raising, a lot of activity having to do with progressive issues. My sister and I were always around a lot of Communists, a lot of different kinds of people.

I was eighteen the first time I went to Alaska. I was living in Seattle with an uncle. My dad was living in California. I was in juvenile prison for a little while. I was really becoming a delinquent. My dad came up from California and said, "I'm going to send you to Alaska." He wanted to show me what he'd gone through and what most of our relatives and other people had gone through. So I thought, "Okay, I'll go." Since he had been the former president of ILWU Local 37, he was able to get me in there. I thought, "I'll just go up for the summertime." And then it just kept going and going, and I ended up going thirty-four years.

There are so many jobs in the cannery. A first-time person has to do what they consider the dirtiest, the worst kind of job. That's sliming—cleaning fish. Almost everybody has to start there and kind of work your way through it. I did that, worked my way up till I got to do a warehouse thing. I was really good with the casing machine, so I ended up doing that for many years. And then, eventually, I became the warehouse foreman, and I was teaching other people to do that.

I was kind of in between the American-born and the immigrants because I was American-born, but raised in the Philippines. So I kind of hung around the *manongs* because I spoke the dialect. I spoke Ilocano. I had sort of an advantage because I could be an American and speak Filipino and understand what was going on.

For coffee breaks, us Filipinos, we were getting just black coffee and a little package of cookies to divide up for the whole crew. The white crew had vegetables, sandwiches, fruits, hot chocolate—I mean, just a banquet, a table full of stuff. We used to tell our foreman, "How come they get all that and we don't?" "That's the way it is. Just be content." Then one day, Gene and other Wapato guys said, "We're going over to the white bunkhouse. Are you comin'?"

And we went and sat down, and then Brindle, the owner, came and said, "Hey, you're not supposed to be in here." Like that. "What do you mean? We work for you. We're going to stay here, and we're going to eat here, too." And then some of the fishermen started coming over. "We're going to break some heads if you guys don't leave here." Gene and I said, "We can break heads, too." So we ended up, they let us eat there. But that was before they reformed everything. That was kind of our way of saying, "Hey, we're not going to stop now."

The older *manongs* would tell me, "No, don't make waves. Just let it go. This is the way it's supposed to be. You stay back." But Gene and the others were real aggressive. I couldn't say, "No, I'm not with you." At first, I was sort of pacified. I had seen it happen before the other guys even came up, but I was just going along with it. It's the way it's always been, so that's the way it's supposed to be. I was interested in my art. I was a hippie at that time. I had other things to do. I wanted to travel. I didn't want to get involved in politics and doing all this stuff. But after Alaska became my only means of living, my support, well, I better do something about it because I want to keep going with it. It's not something that I do for the summer and then just take off and forget. So the longer I stayed there, the more involved I got.

And then people started electing me to shop steward. I would win the election overwhelmingly. I became shop steward for over ten years, and so I had to really do the union work. I had to get involved because I was responsible for all of us. I had to represent them. They had shop stewards up there that were totally company men. You do what you're told. You're shop steward, but you really don't do anything. I had to confront the company, I had to confront the troublemakers, everything. It was a lot of work besides working physically, doing a lot of work, too.

After all of that work the reformers did, if you were still going to Alaska, you could see the difference in the treatment we were getting, the housing, the food. Things actually changed. The crews also changed. Everybody became younger. All the old *manongs* just disappeared, and everything changed, but the conditions were better. A lot of people that were first-timers up there, they had no idea what was before them. They get there and they have a nice bunkhouse. They got good food. They have no idea.

I have always been interested in art, ever since I was a child. I was always drawing, carving, doing something. It all started in the Philippines because it opened up my imagination, coming from the U.S., going to a whole different culture, a whole different way of life. It opened me up, and I'm really grateful that my dad sent me to the Philippines.

Gene was like a real brother. He was direct and up front and honest. He knew about my past drug problems and all that. He didn't use that against me, where some other people did. We could talk about anything. He had planned to come to Mexico and visit me and work on my artwork. We had all kinds of plans, things we were going to do.

You know, my last few years in Alaska, my last six years were up in Dillingham in cold storage and that was really torture for me at that time, being over fifty and having to do that kind of work. It was different, a lot different than it was with Gene and them, with that crew. We had more going. We had bad times and good times.

Bruce Occena

A founding member of the Union of Democratic Filipinos, Bruce came from the San Francisco Bay Area to help establish a KDP chapter in Seattle. He went to Alaska for the first time in 1978 with Silme Domingo and Alonzo Suson with the intent of continuing to organize every season until the union was completely reformed.

My father had been a migrant worker and had come up through California to Washington following the crops, then went to Alaska. In a lot of Filipino families, there is a sense that they need to protect us from that hardship. It wasn't often told. So the irony for me is, later, I'm up as an organizer, trying to organize them, then having a discussion with my father and saying, "We are trying to do this thing." And then he said, "Oh, yeah. What cannery are you working in?" I said, "Uganik." "Oh. I was in this one and that one." I said, "Are you trying to tell me you've never told me you were up there?" So my first introduction to the canneries was through people like Gene and Silme. I was thinking, "This has nothing to do with me." But a couple of years later, I find out it does have something to do with me. I wasn't aware of it at the moment, but actually, my father had been an Alaskero as well.

The canneries were extremely isolated, some more than others. There is no road to Uganik. You'd fly into Kodiak, and it's not like you then get in a truck and go to Uganik. You have to get into small planes and get dropped there. You're literally dropped into nowhere.

The Filipino men at that time had a bunkhouse that was unabashedly called "the Filipino bunkhouse," meaning the white guys didn't have to live there. It's an old barracks type of situation with 1930s beds, these cast-iron beds with mattresses this thin, an old itchy blanket, and a pillow. And then every three, two feet between, a bunk. And it just goes on for fifteen on one side and fifteen on the other. You put your stuff under the bed. This is your bed. And

then there's another bunkhouse where the white workers are that's kind of like a college dormitory.

There's an unspoken rule, but basically, the Filipinos are not allowed. This was the 1970s. My God! It was like a flashback. We knew there was inequality, but personally, I was stunned. I expected inequality, but it would be a little bit more subtle than this. It was sobering. There was not a sign that said, "Filipinos are not allowed in this bunkhouse," but it was clear that that was the way. We had our own bunkhouse. And, in fact, the Eskimos had their own bunkhouse. So it was very carefully segregated.

And then there was an unspoken rule that the different racial groups were not to go into each other's space. The majority of the workers are Filipino males. They have us stacked like it's a military camp. As the season goes on, we have probably forty, fifty young and old Filipino men. We're working at that time, at the peak, literally eighteen hours a day. We had two washing machines. Again, this was the 1970s. So you looked at these washing machines, thinking, "Boy, I haven't seen a washing machine like that in I don't know how long." We had two for all the Filipino workers. After you work eighteen hours, then you have to clean your clothes. You have to get in line and negotiate when it's your turn to throw your clothes in the washing machine.

In the shop itself, I was a slimer because it was my first season there. That was the starting point. Silme was a big shot. He was a butcher. Alonzo and I were slimers. As slimers, the fish would come to us, we'd cut their fins off, and then we split and cleaned them out. But the butchers are the ones who get the fish first. They cut the heads off.

There were a lot of safety issues. I can't even begin to describe them. I know each of us were trying to look at what were the possible safety issues we could organize around. I look back and it still stuns me. You'd be walking, and there'd be a hole in the floor. You'd look right down into the water. Nothing that says, "Watch out. There's a hole in this floor."

There were food safety issues. They would bring in a bin of fish, and sometimes the fish were beautiful. And sometimes in the peak of the season, too many boats came in, so there are fish sitting. By the time we're processing it, it stinks, literally stinks. So then, we're trying to figure out, "Is this an organizing issue?" There's a food problem here, on top of everything else. That's not even a worker safety issue. That's not even an inequality issue. That's kind of a—we didn't even know what the word was—kind of a food ethics issue. I don't know. Can you do this? Those were the kinds of questions we would have in these discussions. Can they pack rotten fish? And of course the response was no response.

The only people we could talk to were the Filipino foremen, and they were all more or less in cahoots. So you run into a brick wall there. It's not like you have access to the people really running the cannery. The racial stratification was so severe that if you were a white worker there, you probably at some point could go and talk to someone running the cannery. But if you were Filipino, your only access was to your Filipino overseers. That's where the union corruption gets in. You go to the Filipino overseer, and it starts there.

I remember about the rotten fish. "Oh, it's okay. It's no problem because we cook it, so all the bacteria get killed in the cooking process." But some of the fish we put in there were green. We'd keep track. People would write on the wall the batches that we knew were good fish because at the end of the season, we got to take some fish home. "I want the fish from these batches." We knew that someone would remember, "Oh, that's a good batch." You wouldn't just take any fish home with you. You had to make sure you took it from the batches that were good.

The funny story I have about Uganik is that we would meet before our shifts, Silme and I.

I stress the isolation of Uganik, but it's beautiful. It's pristine. So there was a pier that we would walk and get some exercise. We'd walk to the end of the pier and back, be engaged in some kind of discussion about some issue that might be an organizing issue, a reform issue. Then we looked up and there was a giant bear, maybe six feet from us. And the bear looked deceptively close because we were on the pier, and then there's a gully. I guess bears can jump. I don't know. I'm a city boy, so I never expected to encounter a bear in real life who wasn't in a zoo. It looked like it could just jump over that six feet and come and eat us up. It growled at us because, I guess, we scared the bear. So here we were—to the extent we thought we were important organizers, we were going to change this industry—the two of us were just like two little kids running, screaming, running down the pier. The bear ran away from us, so we scared each other. That's one of my lasting memories.

Another memory is the way that the hierarchy of the cannery went. The top status was the butchers. If you were Filipino, that's as far as you could get. So Silme was already a big shot. Alonzo and I were just slimers. That's where the Eskimos were, too. So the Filipinos and Eskimos were more or less at the lowest jobs. One of the things Alonzo and I had to figure out was how to make friends with the Eskimos. So we started to remember their names, talk to them about what villages they came from, and in the course of that, breaking that kind of separation among the minorities.

They invited us to their *muk'ee*, their hot steam, which was very significant because you don't go into the *muk'ee* unless you're invited. People told us that Filipinos had never been invited to a *muk'ee* with the Eskimos, so Alonzo and I broke that. After our shifts, they would say, "Come over to the *muk'ee*," and we would go right in there like we were Eskimos and it was wonderful. It's something between a steam and a sauna, very, very nice. We had these strange discussions with the Filipino old-timers. "Careful of those Indians," they would say. We'd say, "You don't even know these guys' names. You've been coming up here for how many years?" "They're Indians." "No, they're not Indians. They're Eskimos."

To me, the real heroism is from the people on the front line, Terri and Angel and Alonzo and David. Those are the people that had to go back and turn the key and open up the union and get ready for the next dispatch when the dispatcher had just been killed. No one ever sets out to be a hero. You're just trying to do what's right, and then circumstance puts something in front of you. And so ordinary people wind up doing extraordinary things. Then later, the mythology is that they were extraordinary people. We've always said, "No,

actually, it was nothing. It was extraordinary events." All of the middle ground gets lost in a crisis like that. There's no middle ground, there's no equivocating. Either you stand up again or you run away.

When I look back and think, given that we were all in our twenties, how did we ever manage to convince each other that we had this backing to go back and do that? Once we did that, a lot of community support came. But it's very important to be clear that that community support only came when a couple of key people right on the front line said to Baruso, "Okay, now you're really in trouble. You think you were in trouble before. You have not seen anything yet." Once that was clear, then all kinds of community support started to come. It was a small group of us who said, "Okay, this is what we're doing." Then they came and said, "You guys are incredible. What can I do?"

The support was crucial after that because we went up against some incredible power. One is the power of the gangs. These were the actual guys who pulled the trigger, and they were dangerous. We would go into union meetings. We knew they were packing, but we were not. It's like these really key tense meetings where you'd hear "click, click." Oh, we know what that "click, click" means. Then Terri or somebody would have to get up and say something after you've just heard all the guns clicking.

We had to get a bigger political protection ring so that we wouldn't have to resort to a gunfight at the union hall. Even though we could hear the guns engage, it was like, "Okay, so you killed two of us. But if you are stupid enough to actually pull one of those guns, you won't get out of this union. You'll go straight to the penitentiary."

Andy Pascua

Andy was a lifelong friend of Gene Viernes from the tight-knit community of Wapato; both wrestled for the high school team. Andy and Gene began working in Alaska in 1966. As "Wapato boys," their experience with hard labor in the fields kept them going through the arduous cannery season. Andy became a plaintiff in the discrimination class action lawsuits filed against the Alaska canneries. He currently works as assistant director for the University of Washington's Office of Minority Affairs & Diversity. Andy gave the eulogy at the funeral for Gene.

Wapato was the only land that Filipinos could own because of the Alien Land Act. It was on the Indian reservation. Chief Joe Charlie sold it to some of our community pioneers, so people started settling there.

When we were nine, ten years old, we started working on the farms. And by the time we were twelve, thirteen, we were seasoned workers, picking up crews and running equipment and all that. And then Alaska was seen as, believe it or not, an easier job because we did outrageous hours on the farm because you owned the farm. You don't just harvest like the migrant crews. You have to be there before them. You have to be there after them. You have to drive it to the warehouse. So by the time we were twelve, thirteen years old, we weren't going home at night. We were sleeping in the packing sheds. So Alaska wasn't working in 105-degree heat in the middle of the summer. It was an indoor job.

You made more money, and it seemed like easier work. You got to remember, too, that we were a community where you helped everyone. Our father used to loan us out like tools. "Oh, I got to harvest my corn." "Well, take my boys." And then we would go to work. If we got paid, that was great. If we didn't get paid, well, that's how it went, too. But Alaska was a real job where they would give you a paycheck. My father and a lot of the men in the community

went in the summers. Gene and I went when we were fifteen. By then, we had been working a few years, so we knew what we were doing.

Someone in the community would get a call and say they're going to dispatch the crew. Then we would drive to Seattle, and we would get our dispatch money, like a forward payment. We gave away a trunk load of vegetables plus some cash for somebody's birthday that we'd never heard of. Found out later it was bribes. But that's okay, because we made more money. So my father got me on and then some cousins of mine and then my younger brother. If we heard it was going to be three days, we'd go back home. If we had to stay around to catch the flight, then we stayed in the International District (ID). That was our experiences in the hotels. You'd take your luggage with you to the restroom, and at night, you'd pile it in front of the door.

Seattle was like Disneyland to us. It was strange because the ID is Asian. We come from Wapato, but we didn't really have an Asian identity. And so the whole ID was exotic and foreign to us even though we were Filipino. We spent what little money we had buying little tourist stuff. We'd wander around and go into the gambling dens just so we could be searched, like we were top-level gangsters. We would be at the Tai Tung as soon as it opened to get *hum bow* or something. We'd go to the Kokusai Theater and spend the day eating our *hum bow* and laughing at the screen because we couldn't understand most of it. It never occurred to us to do any cultural activities like a museum. We did other stuff. We just ran around in a little group until it was time to head to Sea-Tac and head out. The adventures of country boys in the city.

Our crew was a lot of Wapato guys. Eventually, being a Wapato boy was like a status symbol because we came from the farms and we knew how to work and we didn't complain. So a lot of the crews wanted Wapato boys on them. Plus, every crew had two or three old men who could no longer work. So some of our crew, they would help us. They would bring coffee, things like that, but they couldn't work. So we were always working short-handed.

My first year, I was a bin boy. I was up with my dad, and all these salmon come down this conveyor belt very quickly off the boats. And we would sort them into the five species of salmon, and we'd throw them into these giant bins behind us. They would be kept there until they went to the butchering machines. My second year or third year, I became a butcher because it paid more and you operated the butchering machine, the Iron Chink. They'd come out of this big bin, and you would have someone next to you line up and flip the salmon

so they were all facing the same way. I'd pass them from my right hand to my left hand, and seventy times a minute, I would shove the fish into the blade. If you were off or if you were distracted—it was an open blade. It was like a sword. It was scary at first. I would be standing back and throwing the fish. Eventually, you got the rhythm down, but after twenty hours, you'd lose your timing.

There was institutionalized racism. We always were troubled by it, but our fathers and our uncles would tell us, "Don't cause trouble." But it was very hard. And then Uncle Felix passed away, so Gene was up there without his father. My father was still there. Some of the other guys, they didn't have their fathers there.

So we started talking back because they would blackmail us with our fathers' and our families' livelihood. "You do this and none of you are coming back next year." Our fathers would say, "You're wrecking it for everybody. Just keep quiet." Our union rep was one of the uncles from Wapato, so they would use the cultural stuff to try and control us. "You're being disrespectful to Uncle. Why would you do that?" We said, "No, we're trying to enforce the contract." And so that was really difficult because the first hurdle was against our own people, and we didn't like that.

We knew there would be repercussions from our food strike. The way Alaska works is they have fishing, and then the authorities close down the fisheries for a few days to let some salmon through. We'd just worked a real long stretch, three or four days at twenty hours a day. We're all really tired. We basically had a day where we could have a day off, but we were still under contract, and we were saying, "We want some of that food. We know it's there." They said no.

And then they had "make work." What they would have us do on these kinds of days—imagine a gigantic warehouse with metal for canning. We'd move the boxes, hundreds of big cartons full of metal, from one side of the warehouse to the other side. And then the next day, we would move it back. It was simply because they didn't want to pay us without us working. It was a harassment-type thing. And so people were angry. We said, "You know what? We're not going to the warehouse today, not until we get better food." Gene became the spokesperson because they weren't going to get to him because Uncle wasn't there.

I remember one time, one guy managed to smuggle a gun in his luggage into Alaska. There were always grizzly bears around. We weren't always bright. He convinced us to be like beaters on a tiger hunt, to beat the bushes with these little sticks and drive the grizzly bear to him so he could shoot it. Thank God we didn't see any grizzly bears because they would have just eaten us. We were walking back to camp, and we told him, "There's a tree, a little tree. Shoot the tree." All day long, we wanted to hear the gun. He pulled out his gun and he emptied that sucker. Never hit the tree once. And we just looked at him, and we took our sticks and beat him senseless. We thought, "You almost got us all killed, you idiot!"

Another time, there was a big cliff, maybe 150 feet high, and we spent the whole day digging footholds and handholds into this cliff to climb it. You got up there and you got scared because we were way up there. The handholds got deeper and deeper until we were climbing by shoving our entire arms into some hole and then going to the next one. It was just stuff that we would make up. Stan Viernes and I sat on the dock one time almost the whole day, fishing for salmon, until some fisherman took pity on us and told us that salmon don't eat on the way upriver.

After the season ended, when your flight landed at Sea-Tac, you had to check in at the union hall and vote. If you didn't vote, you had to pay the fifty-dollar fine. They deducted it from your next year's pay. We all agreed on the plane that we weren't going to vote. Then our fathers said, "Don't be throwing away fifty dollars. What's wrong with you?" So we went in, and they had this big voting machine. I had never voted before. You threw the levers, and you closed this big lever, and it closed the curtains behind you. We thought, "Wow." So we voted. We purposely voted the wrong way. When you stepped out, you looked at that guy standing behind the machine—the back of the machine was off. They would look at how you voted, and they'd erase your vote so that you wouldn't, you know. I thought, "Oh, great."

The very first thing that Gene and I did that I can recall was our family went to visit his family on the farm. Gene told me that if we mixed vinegar with baking soda, we could make a bomb. We were like seven, eight years old. We spent the whole day stealing stuff from his mom's kitchen so we could make this bomb. He convinced me that it worked because he would throw this bag of baking soda into the air and it would leave a trail and then fall to earth. It was just little things like that. It was the accumulation of a lifelong relationship. He is one of the first people I consciously remember as a person separate from myself because your parents are just considered part of you or whatever. I was so young when we met, and we were born only ten days apart. And then we grew up in the community.

I remember one conversation when we were really young. We were always reading comic books and stuff. He looked at me and said, "Do you ever suspect sometimes that our parents are from outer space?" I was like, "What?" But I knew what he was talking about, that they were so alien to us and they were so different from everyone else in the community, our teachers, all these institutions. They just seemed to have come from someplace completely alien. Even early on, you do realize you're different, so you want to know, "Why is this the way it is?" A lot of the answers are in history.

Gene was very persistent. He would keep after things until he got them. One person's leader is another person's bossy person. As we were growing up, it was a constant battle to tell him, "Quit bossing me around." We were the same age. We both had younger brothers. Gene would come up with this idea, and we would come up with ideas that we thought were equally good. But he was so persistent and he would just wear us down until we said, "Yeah, okay. That makes sense."

He was the kind of guy, we were working and they would say, "I need someone to drive a jitney." We didn't know how to drive a jitney, but he would raise his hand and say, "I'll drive

it." Then he had a new skill. He was always on the edge of the envelope to go one more step. A lot of times, he became the leader because he had that skill or he was willing to take that risk and other people held back.

I remember going down the highway in Seattle. Gene and I were going somewhere. We were forty-five minutes late because he kept stopping for cars that were disabled on the highway. And he had a damn toolbox with him. We would be driving, and there would be somebody disabled. He'd stop and fix their car. I'd say, "C'mon, man. We gotta go." And then there'd be somebody else up the road. They'd need their battery terminal cleaned. He'd stop and fix their car. I'd think, "We're never gonna get there." But his thing was, if we were in Wapato and we saw someone disabled at the side of the road, we would help them. "There's just more of them here. We're still going to stop." It takes forever to get anywhere with him. So after that, I kept saying, "I'll drive. Wave at people or something." But that's who he was. He was always concerned for other people.

He was a leader. He was in the community. He felt the responsibility. There was nothing else he could do. A lot of people asked me that after the murders. "Why didn't he stop? Why are you guys doing this stuff?" And I would think to myself, "How can you not? How can you not be doing this stuff? We were raised in America. We were taught to believe it was a democracy. We were raised in a community that showed respect to its elders. We were raised to believe in one another. How can you not do that?" So it was really hard to explain to them because they were asking me from a place that, no matter how much I talked, they wouldn't understand it. But the way we were raised, that was pretty much going to be the response from us. We were going to tear it down, and he did. So that was very impressive.

Alonzo Suson

Alonzo Suson was born in the Philippines and came to the United States at the age of sixteen. He moved to Seattle two years later and worked for three seasons in the Alaska canneries. A veteran community and labor activist, he currently lives in Phnom Penh, Cambodia.

I worked in Uganik Bay. I was part of the kitchen crew. It was a connection through Tony Baruso and Nemesio Domingo, Silme's father.

So in '78, I got hired as a dishwasher and then worked overtime in the cannery sliming fish with Bruce Occena.

My father knew Silme's mother, and I would call her "auntie." Silme was like an older brother to me. We'd go out drinking. I'd get hand-me-downs from him. "Here's some pants, nice clothes. It's a good fit." Gene was more intellectual, introspective. We were roommates on College Street. They were both very serious at a very young age.

Gene and Silme are now icons, but we knew them as human beings. They were just doing what we were doing. For me now, it's still true that collectively, we can work things out and we can make change. Change is about disliking current conditions, having a vision, taking the first step, and overcoming resistance. I think for me, the legacy of Gene and Silme is that it represents the death of our youth. The demand for justice possibly made them bigger than life. But I knew them as a friend, brother, and roommate. They're admirable people. They did things because of their belief that things can change.

I'm still working with unions, but on an international scale. We've been working in Dhaka, Bangladesh, and for the last six years, in Cambodia. In Cambodia, it's a pretty young trade union. In Bangladesh, it's much older. I can relate to the need for change because of what we did with ILWU Local 37. Linked with that is also the issue of how to deal with murders, because when I first went to Cambodia, a few months earlier, one of the most militant trade union leaders in Cambodia, Chea Vichea, was murdered.

Chea Vichea was a young trade unionist in his late thirties. The trade union movement in Cambodia probably started in the 1980s, and Chea Vichea was also a political activist. He was able to lead one of the trade unions to grow and was very militant in the demands for workers' rights and better conditions in the garment industry in Cambodia. He was very well known and was considered very dangerous for the party in power. So how did people react after his murder? Just looking at how we reacted when Silme and Gene were killed, I think there was just a lot of things missing. I could see how things have developed and what things could have been done.

The average age of Cambodian labor leaders is in the thirties. Their union experience probably is five to seven years. I have a good time teaching about change, about power. And so now, my advice to people, especially youth, is that it's all about power. It's not just doing things. There's also studying it so that we understand how to make a change. And to do it with peers, not just by yourself. You debate, you discuss and exchange ideas and learn from each other. But all of this is nothing if you don't got power—you're not able to change things. The most important thing is it's about people. People are power.

Emily Van Bronkhorst

In high school, Emily was greatly influenced by her older sister, a women's rights activist at the University of Washington, and her mother, who was involved in social justice work at their church. In 1975, she began working for the Northwest Labor and Employment Law Office (LELO), where she worked for four years on the Alaska Cannery Workers Association lawsuits. Gene Viernes later recruited her to go to Alaska to organize for the Rank-and-File Committee of Local 37. She is currently executive vice president of SEIU Healthcare 1199NW.

The LELO office was a hotbed of progressive and radical political activity. I was familiar with the United Farm Workers from the grape boycott, but the United Construction Workers Association and the Alaska Cannery Workers Association (ACWA) were both new to me. It was new and exciting, and I loved going to work there.

The ACWA plaintiffs were active in helping work on the cannery lawsuits. That's how I met Terri Mast, Gene Viernes, and Silme and Nemesio Domingo. My work was reading depositions and documents of cannery workers relating their gruesome work experiences in the canneries for the *Domingo v. New England Fish Company* lawsuit, the first to go to trial. I noted where workers testified about the existence of a "Filipino bunkhouse" or the "white mess hall" and the casual way that overtly racist and demeaning words like "flip jobs" were the normal language of management and supervisors, who were all white.

It was pretty shocking and also business as usual in the canneries. The testimony of managers and supervisors detailed the segregation as a fact of life, but they would add that the good jobs were open to everyone, they didn't discriminate. Except they never thought there were any qualified Filipinos to be beach gang workers or machinists. I also knew from testimony that white women worked in the egg

house, ate in the white mess hall, and were hired outside of the union dispatch, getting jobs through a management connection.

Occasionally, Terri or Gene would come into the office and work with me tracking down witnesses and charting testimony. We discussed union and civil rights, feminism, and the struggle in the Philippines. I went with Gene to a demonstration outside the Philippine consulate to mark the anniversary of the declaration of martial law in the Philippines. I was impressed with how serious and organized he was. Gene was always asking, "What's your goal here?" about anything I was working on.

Gene was very detail-oriented. The summer of 1979, he enrolled in a labor studies program and came back all fired up. He gave Terri and me a long list, two pages, single-spaced, with his ideas for delegate training for Local 37. It was so long and so involved, we just laughed. We couldn't believe that he wanted us to put all that history into a two-hour training class. He thought we could do it, and should do it.

Gene and I shared a love of sports. He was a real jock, right down to wearing his Wapato letter jacket, which made him stand out in a crowd of political activists. We used to go for runs and play Frisbee or football. Gene liked to party as much as anyone. He had some favorite taverns on Beacon Avenue that had Pac-Man and pool tables. He liked to drink beer and burp real loud. He thought it was funny that he could make more noise that way than anyone else.

After I left LELO, I worked in a warehouse, and then as a painter at Seattle University. We organized our maintenance crew into the International Longshore and Warehouse Union (ILWU) Local 9, the Seattle warehouse union, and I was on the first bargaining committee. Gene would come by our paint shop to give us encouragement.

Gene constantly talked to me about going up to Alaska. He said I should put all the "book knowledge" about working in the Alaskan canning industry toward helping out the Rank-and-File Committee (RFC). So I got recruited in that way. I had already joined the KDP as an associate member, attending events and meetings.

So, I finally went down to the union hall to get dispatched in the spring of 1980. Silme told me to "dress up" and not to wear my painter overalls. Silme scared the hell out of me. He wore black clothes with platform heels, a black brimmed hat. He kind of barked at people, had a real loud laugh, and engaged everyone in conversation.

I was dispatched to Diamond E Fisheries plant in Egegik. Both Terri Mast and Lynn Domingo worked there before, knew the crew, the gangsters, the white women, the *manongs*, and pro-RFC members. My job, as instructed by Terri and Gene, was to build a diverse grievance committee to support the delegate in resolving problems, and to organize for the slate of reform candidates. I had my stack of *Alaskero News* to hand out, and instructions on how to sign up the white workers to join the union. Terri repeatedly warned me about some of the crew there, including Jimmy Ramil, known to be gangsters.

The work was hellish, first on the "patching table" then on the "slime line." It was cold, wet, dirty work, really long hours. I was used to working hard, but factory work was new. I ate in the Filipino mess hall, worked on the Filipino crew, and stayed in the women's bunkhouse. The men's bunkhouse was really old, holes in the floor, cold, just a real pit. About halfway through the season, Gene and Silme visited Diamond E on their tour of canneries to make sure that management was respecting the contract to sign up workers into the union, and to campaign for their election. I have never been so glad to see friends as when they walked up the boardwalk. I remember crying to Gene about how horrible it was, and him essentially saying, "Buck up, Em."

At the end of the summer, all the RFC

candidates won election. Silme was re-elected secretary-treasurer. Gene was now the dispatcher. We were looking forward to implementing our plans in the next season.

Gene's commitment to his work was pretty all-consuming, and his trip to the Philippines was something he really looked forward to. The first time I saw him after his 1981 trip was in Hawaii at the ILWU convention. He was really ragged and worn out after traveling and leading the fight to pass the resolution on Philippine solidarity. He couldn't even enjoy an afternoon at the beach. He was too worried and told us he had been under surveillance.

I left the union hall on June 1 around 4 P.M. I had met with Gene to talk about when we were going to have a RFC meeting. Around 5 P.M., I got a phone call from Leni in the KDP, telling me Gene had died in the union hall, and that Silme was taken to Harborview and that I needed to stay at home. We all went to the union hall over the next weeks to try to maintain the fair dispatch and to keep the union running.

In late June, Alonzo Suson and I were sent to Alaska by the executive board to try to organize a large group of cannery workers in Cordova. Silme had started Local 37's engagement with ILWU Local 200 and they needed our help to win an election. Alonzo and I spent three weeks trying to build a committee and organize a thousand cannery workers in Cordova. The companies jumped on the murders and posted flyers in all the plants saying the union was corrupt. We lost badly.

Over the next seven years, we organized in Kenai, Homer, and Seward and tried to build our union with cannery workers who had no experience with a union. The turnover from year to year was incredibly high.

I learned from Gene that you have to have a strong organizing committee. That's what will build a real organization: a strong group of leaders, working together. I think the Rank-and-File Committee did that.

Velma Veloria

In 1992, Velma was elected to the Washington State Legislature, making her the highest-ranking elected official of Filipino ancestry in the United States at the time. She was also the first Filipina American, first Asian American, and first woman ever elected to the Washington State Legislature. She served for twelve years.

I came to Seattle in August 1984. I was sent up to Alaska in September, where I worked for the summer and fall. It was a big change for me. King Cove was the farthest point I could have gone, coming from New York. I worked two seasons. One moment, I was a medical technician in New York working with test tubes and test samples, and the next minute, I was working with salmon as a patcher in a cannery. For me, New York was high fashion and international finance and high-level stuff. I came here and all I saw were people in wool and flannel shirts. I thought, "Oh, my God! This is their fashion?" I tried to figure out how to adjust from a fast-paced environment to a sleepy town.

What I enjoyed about Alaska was that, in the brief time that you're together—in those six weeks you're up there—the workers, they become your family. Before I worked in Alaska, I had never worked with other manual laborers. I was used to working with professionals like doctors, nurses, office workers. Here I was, working on an assembly line, putting in a little dab of salmon to fill these cans. It was a humbling experience. At first, I was scared because most of the people in the canneries were men. But I overcame that and learned how to hang out with them. I even learned how to drink vodka and orange juice.

I was sent here by the Union of Democratic Filipinos, the KDP. They felt that the Filipino cannery workers were instrumental in getting word back and forth about what was happening in the Philippines under martial law. The KDP had been working toward an interna-

tional strike against all goods coming from the Philippines, but that plan got diverted when Silme and Gene were murdered.

I immigrated here when I was eleven years old, but I just didn't see my future in the Philippines anymore. My relatives in the Philippines had already left. By this time, they were in California. The break for me was really realizing that I couldn't have one foot in one place and the other foot in another place. Once I made that decision, I went ahead with investing my energy and passions in doing what I could to change the system in this country.

On January 18, 1992, I wrote in my diary, "I am going to run for office to declare that this country is my home." Jesse Jackson was running for president, and he was talking about issues that I cared passionately about. When I ran for a position in the state legislature, I had a struggle because, in the eyes of the KDP, I had become part of the enemy. They didn't support me running for electoral office. But the way I saw it, I was way ahead of my time. I found my support base in the broader Asian American community and the African American community.

By the time I declared my intention to run for office, the KDP had disbanded. The Marcos dictatorship was already gone. Many of us were getting older. Some of us wanted to get pregnant and raise families. Many of us moved into the broader peace and social justice movements. A lot of us went into union work. Some became academicians.

Silme and Gene gave me the strength to fight for peace and social justice. I think about them—and the fact that they gave up their lives. If they can give up their lives, I'm going to do what I can to contribute to a better world. My life—as I moved forward into a position as a state legislator—became about supporting all that they stood for, whether it's combating human trafficking, standing up for immigrant and worker rights, or fighting for social justice.

Conan Viernes

A Wapato native, Conan is the first-born son of Stan and Gloria Viernes. He was two years old when his uncle, Gene Viernes, was killed. Conan is a program analyst for the University of Washington's Office of Minority Affairs & Diversity in Toppenish, Washington.

The only real memory I have of Uncle Gene is when he gave me some backpacks from the Philippines. There was excitement, and I thought my parents were excited for the backpacks. But they were actually excited for the comic book inside the backpack because my name is Conan, and it was the first Conan comic book. But as a child, I didn't really care about the comic book. I liked the backpack. It was a straw backpack, custom-made. I had never seen one from the Philippines.

My family tells me about a lot of different times that I spent with Uncle Gene. One in particular is when, at his funeral, I looked down at him in the casket. I said, "Uncle Gene looks cold. Let's get him a blanket." For some reason, that really sticks with me.

Uncle Gene was a complex person. I see this side of him that's the Viernes side, the rough and tough. But I also have this side of Gene that's the very professional, very outspoken, does what he thinks needs to be done to right the wrongs and to stick up for little people who don't necessarily have a voice. I kind of see that in myself sometimes, like there's a part of me that is from Wapato, born and raised here. The outside world is kind of scary. And then, when I get into the outside world, I feel like I'm a proponent for speaking the truth.

I think what Uncle Gene has inspired in me is to always seek the truth. You don't necessarily need to convince other people of the truth, but always look deeply at issues, find out what is my truth in these issues, and move toward that truth.

Stan Viernes

Stan was born eighteen months after his brother, Gene. The Viernes brothers spent their early years on family farms in the Wapato area. After he turned sixteen, Stan began working in the Alaska salmon canneries with Gene and their father, Maximo Felix Viernes. At Central Washington University, Stan studied economics and business. He has worked for many years at the Yakima County Juvenile Court, most recently as a probation counselor.

Alaska was a connection to family and friends. It was a point of pride being one of the Wapato boys, that they'd call us first and last. We would be there, start it up, finish it up. You had to keep up, shoulder to shoulder kind of a thing. As hard as it was, it was just a matter of pride, just to do the same work your parents did, or your uncles. You'd be protective of them, to realize how hard they worked. When we were up there, they were in their 60s. They were still working hard. How can you quit when you have sixty-year-old men doing the same work as you? You just don't dare quit.

I was real close to my dad. I just loved him. I could really appreciate his life story, coming from the Philippines when he was sixteen, seventeen, the first in his family to go to America. He worked the migrant trails, and Alaska was part of that. Gene went to Alaska two years before me. I remember being very impressed because Gene was my older brother, but he never really seemed like my big brother because I was bigger than him. When he went up to Alaska alongside my dad, I was just so impressed with that. I remember the day they came home from the first season. I was just staring at him in awe. He was passed out on the couch. When I went up, I was glad to. It was a connection to our dad. It was an honor to go up there with him.

My dad cared so much about his family. He worked hard to keep us in food and clothes. I just really appreciate that. He worked grave-yard at a warehouse in Selah, a town up north. He would come home and he would have breakfast ready for us. Then he'd go out and work in the fields for a while. Then he'd come home and go to sleep. We didn't see a lot of him, but when we saw him, it was just a real close relationship.

My first year I went up there, I was a slimer. It was a pretty set schedule. You'd start to work by four o'clock. You'd work till six o'clock, go to breakfast, come back, work till lunch, come back, work till dinner, come back, work till clean-up time. So you'd be there till midnight sometimes. And then you go back and go to sleep in the bunkhouse for four hours and start again. So it was just kind of repetitive, every day during the run. We worked seven days a week, twenty hours a day. It was hard. You're wet. You're cold. But it was sharing history with my dad. The hard work was bonding. It was pride that you could do it. How many sixteen-year-olds could say they were up in Alaska sliming for twenty hours a day?

My second year, I was in charge of the bins up on top, bringing the fish in these huge bins. They were probably as big as this room, each bin. There'd be eight of them. They'd be filled with fish to the top, and my job was to get them onto a conveyor belt. They had little levers that you'd [pull to] open up the doors, and the fish would come out, and they would drop on the conveyor belt. I'd feed that conveyor belt and then feed another one up onto the butchering tables. Well, the machinery was really old. If you loaded it up too much, it would freeze up. I got to where I could get that slew of fish just moving perfectly. Well, at one point, they were going really fast, and one of the machines had run out of fish.

The head butcher came up, just yelling and screaming and pushed me aside and said, "Here!" He started loading the belt up, and it froze and the whole production went down. Brindle, the owner of the company, was an older gentleman who was just really hard-nosed. He saw that production was shut down, and he came running up there. The head butcher took off running, and the owner came over. He was yelling at me, pointing his fingers at me. My dad was working up at the top of the bins and saw what had happened. He came sliding out of the rafters and just landed right between me and that old man. He says, "It's not my son's fault. It was that man's fault there. Don't yell at my son." And the owner, who was a very powerful man, just took off. He was scared of my dad because he jumped down like Tarzan, coming out of the rafters.

I started when I was sixteen, going up there with my dad. Then he passed away, worked himself to death. I stopped going because Dad was my connection to Alaska. I was twenty, Gene was twenty-one and a half, and, basically, he kept me home. I helped raise my younger brothers and sisters, so I was the Wapato Viernes and Gene was the "out in the world" Viernes. He tried to keep me separated from that. He knew I was raising a family. He respected that, and I respected him. When he came into the valley, it wasn't about Alaska so much. It was about family and what we needed, what he needed.

Gene and I got slightly separated once. I remained in junior high school. He went up to high school. I kind of lost track of him for about six or seven months. We were at a basketball game one night, and one of my friends said, "Why don't we go down to the high school? It's about six or seven blocks away. They're having a wrestling match." I thought, "That would be interesting." So we went to the wrestling match.

In those days, Wapato had a real huge gym. We got there and the lights were out. The wrestling mat was in the center of the floor. They had a huge light that came down. It was like a spider light. The mat was lit up and everything else was dark. And they started announcing the wrestling match. The opposing team was lined up. They started to introduce the wrestlers. Well, all of a sudden, this big spotlight was showing right up there at the opening of the locker rooms. And they said, "Wrestling from Wapato, sophomore, sixteen, Gene Viernes!" I go, "I didn't even know he was on the wrestling team."

He steps out in the spotlight and he's got the coolest uniform on. He's got white shoes with black stripes. He's got white headgear, a black wrestling outfit with a satin gold top with a big "W" on it. And he runs out there, 103-pounder. I didn't know he was a wrestler. That was the first year he wrestled. I don't know if he won, but Gene was enormous after that. Like I said, he wasn't my big brother. He was my little brother, my older brother. But after that, he was enormous. That inspired me. I joined wrestling the next year, the first year they had it in junior high.

Steve Viernes

A younger brother of Gene Viernes, Steve worked on small family-owned ranches in the Yakima Valley and in the Alaska canneries in the 1970s and early 1980s. He was a plaintiff in the New England Fish Company lawsuit and became one of the first Filipinos to work as a machinist in the canneries. He worked for sixteen years as a mill-wright and maintenance foreman for Longview Fiber Company before becoming an electrician for Sonoco Products Company in Wapato.

I was probably in the sixth grade. That was the first time Gene really started to talk to me about mechanical things. He was a senior, and he had one of the fastest cars in the region. He could work on them and keep them really well tuned. We'd rebuild them. I'd work with him and we'd talk a lot. He'd explain a lot of things. I'm learning all this stuff and helping him—tools, everything. So that stuff all came into play later in my career. That was the first time I really got to see how you use your mind and think in different ways and really pick things apart. He would tear things apart like you wouldn't believe, just so he could put them back together. We'd do that a lot.

Ever since I can remember, my dad was going up to Alaska. As the brothers got older, he'd start taking them with him, too, until he passed away. He never really talked much about that. He was a pretty reserved man. I really don't know the first year he went, but he went up there quite a bit, and we were always anxious for him to get back. When you're so young, you didn't know what they were doing. You just knew they were gone, far away.

A lot of people went when they were really young, fifteen. Well, the summer I was going to turn fifteen, my father passed away, so I never did go after that. And then, in the later years, my last name became more difficult to get up there because of Gene's work. The first year I went was 1978. Silme actually helped me get to where he had worked. It was through the

union, but it was more through the management. Tony Diaz was the foreman then and, basically, put in a good word, and in our dispatch, they needed some workers. I was on the list and my name came up. I filled retorts all summer long at the New England Fish Company in Uganik Bay on Kodiak Island.

As the salmon is coming off and being put into the retort baskets, they're stacking them up, and then the minute they're full, our job was to put every one of them baskets in the oven as they came off. There were three lines, and so we were just going back and forth, back and forth. You bulked up pretty quick because those things weighed a lot. And so that's all I did all day long, from eight in the morning until sometimes three the next morning, just going back and forth and unloading and loading, just a lot of physical hard labor. The work was just so repetitive. Some people didn't like doing that, but it was okay for me. The day went fast. You'd get done; you'd be pretty exhausted.

Gene got me involved because of what I was doing in Alaska. They were keeping a lot of Filipinos out of jobs, saying they weren't qualified. But when I went up and I poked into a lot of the jobs that they were saying you can't do, he wanted to use me as an example. Stuff I learned from him when I was young helped me out later on, along with growing up around farms. You had to be able to do a lot of different things. I became a machinist, working year-round for the canneries. So in the wintertime, I would be overhauling and tearing equipment apart and putting them all back together and getting them into shape and then going up and installing them and getting them all ready and then maintaining them. It was a lot of hours, more than what the cannery workers were doing.

I had fun just shooting water and washing stuff down. I would take my time so I wouldn't be bored. If the equipment was running, I would make myself busy. I might grab hoses and wash it down just to pass the time. Sometimes in my

job, you could fall asleep pretty easy. You didn't want to, because usually the crews that were working there would make your life miserable by jamming stuff because they wanted a break. I would get up and help others, just whatever it took to keep moving and making the day go. I never got injured. Growing up around farm equipment, you just learn to watch your hands and all around you and be aware. That stuff in Alaska is pretty dangerous.

I could see some of the problems that were at the canneries, and I got to see it change, so I knew what the reformers were doing was working. I used to see Gene's pictures when he'd come back. "Why did you take a picture of that?" It must have been a plan. He had that plan long before, because he really kept quiet for quite a while because of our father. He didn't want to make big waves. When my father died, that changed it. It freed him up, so he started moving in that direction. He ended up going to Seattle for what he was doing.

Michael Woo

Michael has spent a lifetime building multiracial partnerships and mobilizing communities. In 1970, he joined the United Construction Workers Association and fought for the racial integration of Seattle's unionized construction industry. A founding board member of Legacy of Equality, Leadership, and Organizing, he later served as codirector until 2006. He is now director of the Seattle start-up Got Green.

My dad did not work in Alaska, but he knew a lot of the men in Chinatown that were part of the ILWU Local 37 that went every summer to go work in the salmon canneries. One of them was a man named Bing. He was a Woo. He was my distant uncle. My dad knew Gene Navarro. He told me when I was in high school, if I wanted to go work in Alaska, I could. I was a little afraid of that because I didn't know anybody that was going. But he took me down there, and Uncle Bing took me in, introduced me to Navarro. I went through this quick membership process. And that's how I got up to Alaska.

I was a cannery worker at a New England Fish Company cannery in Uganik Bay, and that's where I met Nemesio and Silme. I was sixteen, seventeen. I became friends with them in the cannery. Nemesio worked in the mess hall. He was a waiter, so at every meal, he'd be in the area. I'd get to talk to him, but his hours were different, because in the mess hall, they worked to get ready for breakfast. And then after dinner, they were done.

Silme was a slimer. I was an egg puller. So the way the fish process works is after the beach gang—the white folks—unloaded the boat, the fish would then come down the chute. They'd get sorted, and we'd run different types of fish. The fish that started coming out,

the butchers would line them up and they'd chop the heads off; the Iron Chink chops the heads off. And then I'm the next person there, and I pull the eggs out. I'm really good friends with the Japanese that are there because they want the eggs to be perfect. I was a really good, fast egg puller. I'd pull the skeins out and separate the guts. After that, the fish go to the sliming table. They're cleaning out what didn't get cleaned out. Then they go to the processing line, where they either get cut for canning or they get shipped out. Most of the stuff was cut for canning. Then there's a whole canning process, which is a separate part.

Silme was down the line. We were in the same wet space. When we weren't in the cannery working, we were in the bunkhouse or doing our meals. I was telling my son the other day when we were doing laundry, I just said, "When I was your age, we used to run our laundry through a machine, where it was a wringer. It wasn't automatic." If you were lucky, you had one of the newer ones where you could plug it in. The white bunkhouse, they had all the electric stuff. It didn't take them hours to do their laundry. But we would do laundry together; we would eat together, play cards, sing songs.

I wasn't politicized at sixteen or seventeen. I didn't really learn about the name "Iron Chink" until after I came back. I knew it was called a "Chink." We talked about that in the mess hall, the way young guys talk. The brothers would say, "nigger" this, "nigger" that, "chink" this, "chink" that. I didn't really think about it until I got back. And then, I'm older and I'm working for United Construction Workers. I'm getting more of a political frame. During the discovery process, when all this stuff comes out, I said, "Yeah, I remember that Chink." It became a real issue at that point for me. A lot of the Filipino workers up there, they didn't think nothing of it. I was probably in that same mind-set when I was working up there.

Between Silme and Nemesio, Silme was always a little bit more flamboyant. I don't think Nemesio—he might have had a pair of platform shoes—but Silme definitely had platform shoes. We grew up in that era of platform shoes and big bell-bottoms. We were planning to go out one time, and I'd come to pick him up or he'd pick me up. We'd have on the exact same thing. It's a big issue for girls when guys have the same platform shoes and the same bell-bottoms. It would crack me up. He was famous for his platform shoes and his big, polyester, widespread collar. That's how I'll always remember Silme. And the Monte Carlo. That was his baby.

I hung out with Silme because he was a lot of fun. We grew up in the '70s. We did all of the exploratory drug stuff. We got high together and told a lot of stories. He actually helped to politicize me. He was very smart beyond his years. He knew a lot more about the oppression of workers than anybody would give him credit for.

I was in the class action lawsuit against New England Fish Company. That's why we got this house. The cases were filed in '73. They were litigated in the late '70s. New England Fish Company was the first case to be won. I had forgotten about it. Marie and I were living together in a studio apartment. I had nothing

to my name. Well, somebody called me, saying, "You're going to get a check." It was enough money to buy a car. I said, "C'mon, Marie." We went to Everett to look at this Cadillac convertible. I said, "I want to get this great big Cadillac convertible." She said, "You're not buying that car. We're going to buy a house." I hate to tell Marie she was right, but she was right. It reinforced for me this idea of class action with punitive damages, and it reinforced for me that that stuff could work.

Now we don't have that. The courts have flipped. Those folks that worked at Wards Cove didn't get any of that. That's why we kept fighting. In the early '90s, when there was this national move around resurrecting the Wards Cove stuff, I became active again.

I'm still doing organizing work. I work for an organization called Got Green. It's a group that I helped get started in 2008. We're looking at ensuring that there's equity and opportunity in this green movement. One of the places we started with was green jobs. It has some of the same historical focus where a lot of the construction jobs, the built environment, is being built green now. So the framework is around green jobs and even the same unions that we were tackling in the late '60s, early '70s, around employment discrimination, access to apprenticeship, I'm still tagging that on. What does it mean for low-income, diverse communities? We're doing organizing around that.

PART

3
The Past

"*The old world is dying, but a new world is being born. It generates inspiration from the chaos that beats upon us all.*"

—Carlos Bulosan

AFTERWORD

In 1977, Gene Viernes wrote a seven-part series for the *International Examiner* on the history of the Pacific canned-salmon industry, the role of Asian immigrant laborers, and the development of the cannery workers union.

Gene, a student of the newly developed ethnic studies curriculum in the universities, understood that rediscovering and reinterpreting this history was itself an act of assertive defiance. In the 1970s the histories of marginalized peoples in the U.S. remained an addendum to the "real" history of presidents, captains of industry, and the white upper class. Gene's recovery of these stories set the stage for growing academic interest in Asian American history and Seattle's radical labor history.

As Gene and others began their efforts to reform the union, they drew inspiration from learning that the challenges they faced were not new. They were, as Silme Domingo often described it, part of the ebb and flow of organizing movements that stretched back to—and connected them directly with—the lives of their fathers.

Gene asked me to help turn the *Examiner* series into a stand-alone publication that would allow a wider audience to know this "hidden history." Gene wrote the series quickly, under tight newspaper deadlines. He typed the articles in the office of the Alaska Cannery Workers Association in between organizing meetings. Although Gene would apologetically say he was not a historian and that his articles were "rough," I knew he felt a great sense of pride that he could bring something of value to the historical record.

Many *Examiner* readers said they enjoyed the series. Local families still had a direct connection to the experience, and historians frequently cited the articles. Pleasantly surprised by this interest, Gene and I discussed expanding the series into a book, illustrated with historical images depicting working and living conditions in the Alaska canneries. In one scribbled note, Gene told me he wanted to include recent photos "embodying the humanness, deepness of Filipino personalities, and life experiences."

We discussed how we might add more flesh to the bones of the history. Gene drafted a preface and introduction to the book, neither of which he was happy with; and he admitted that he didn't really know the difference between a preface and an introduction. Laughing, I told him that I didn't know the difference either. We left it there. Gene also intended to update the ending to bring the reader up to present. He never completed those tasks.

The project waited for a time when we could apply ourselves to the research, editing, and rewriting. Sadly, this time never came, and after Gene's death, the incomplete manuscript languished in my basement files.

After the murders, many friends contributed five, ten, or twenty dollars—totaling over $1,000—to help pay for the book's completion. The money came unsolicited, and I was quite touched. I donated the money to the Committee for Justice for Domingo and Viernes, feeling this would be the best use of the funds.

In October 2010, I approached Terri Mast to discuss how we might finally publish Gene's manuscript as part of a larger project recounting the events leading to the murders and the enduring effect of Gene and Silme's lives.

Presented here is Gene's original manuscript, edited for grammar, brevity, and clarity. To help the reader along, I added information on the salmon canning industry and the section that describes the canning process.

In many ways, Gene's manuscript is an artifact of its time, touching only briefly on topics which others have more thoroughly explored since. But it remains a firm starting point for new generations who want to understand the salmon-canning industry and the immigrant pioneers whose blood, sweat, and hearts went into building a union and a better life for those who now follow.

Ron Chew
January 26, 2012

Alaskeros History

By GENE VIERNES

Introduction

April, May, and June bring many new faces to the streets of Seattle's Chinatown. Not only do the trees sprout new leaves, but the city gains new faces. The faces are those of the Alaskeros waiting for dispatch to the Alaska salmon canneries. They come from as far away as California, Oregon, and Idaho. Some are young and have experienced the northward trek only a few times. The older ones are as familiar with the streets of Seattle's Chinatown as they are with those of Stockton, San Francisco, and Los Angeles. They all hope to make a small fortune in the salmon canneries, either to finance another year in school or perhaps just to survive until next spring.

There is silence between generations, only an occasional acknowledgment between a young slimer and an old butcher. Perhaps, the young Alaskero hopes the *manong* will put in a good word about him to the foreman. One might blame this silence on their provincial background or language differences, but what

Cannery workers in Seattle embark for Alaska in 1948.
Carl Camarillo photo. Courtesy International Examiner.

is it really behind this gap between generations? There are many unanswered questions in a young Alaskero's mind. He wants to know why they have to seek work whites refuse to do. He wants to know why Filipinos are segregated from the rest of the cannery crews. The young Alaskero wants to know what the *manongs* mean when they say, "*Bahala na.*"

The *manongs* have lived with their Alaskan experiences for decades. They know the young can't relate to the hardships they experienced under the contract system or the immense pride they felt when they formed a union and ousted the contractors. The "young buffalos" will have to learn for themselves what the *manongs* mean when they say, "It's better now than in the past."

We encourage you to seek out these workers and have them tell you in their own words what it means to have been an Alaskero.

Part I. The Salmon Canning Industry

Salmon, one of the principal fish of the world, live in the rivers and coastal waters of the North Pacific Ocean. There are five species of salmon—all of which were used as a commercial canning product. They are sockeye or red, coho, pink, chum, and chinook. Of the local species of salmon, sockeye was considered the prized species because of its flavor. Historically, salmon runs existed from California up the coast to Alaska and across to Siberia. Salmon spawn in freshwater streams, and their offspring make their way into the sea, where they mature. It is during the yearly runs of the adult salmon back to spawning grounds that the fish are caught in nets and traps and brought to nearby commercial canneries to be prepared for market.

But it wasn't until a method of preserving and packaging seafood was developed that the industry was born. Over the years, the basic methods of canning have been modernized and made more efficient, but they have not changed dramatically. To ensure freshness and minimize waste of fish, most canning facilities are located in proximity to the point of harvest, and crews are brought in perform the arduous work at an assembly line requiring speed, precision, and long hours.

The Pacific West Coast salmon canning industry began with entrepreneur William Hume. In 1852, Hume moved to California to harvest salmon in the Sacramento River. In 1856, he was joined by his brothers, George and John. In the spring of 1864, a friend of George Hume, Andrew Hapgood, brought his canning equipment to California. Together, they established Hapgood, Hume & Co., the first salmon cannery on the West Coast, in Sacramento, California.

In their first year, they produced two thousand cases, each case containing forty-eight one-pound cans. The cans were painted "fiery red," denoting red salmon. They lost half to spoilage, but the remaining half was sold on the Australian market at a profit. This enabled them to pay off past debts and prepare for the season of 1865.

Sediment stirred up by the hydraulic mining upstream prevented salmon from spawning productively and caused Hapgood, Hume & Co. to move north to the Columbia River. In 1866, at Eagle Cliff, Washington, the first Columbia River cannery began operation. The following year, the company dissolved. Each of the Hume brothers and Andrew Hapgood started individual companies.

Industrialization

After the Civil War, others became interested in duplicating the success of the Hapgood, Hume & Co. canneries in California and on the Columbia River.

People moving westward crowded into the Columbia River towns of Oregon and Washington. Competition between cannery operations increased, and cannery owners began looking for new fishing grounds. In 1877, the first Puget Sound cannery was started at Mukilteo by Jackson, Myers & Co. By 1881, Columbia River canneries were producing 630,000 cases.

Cannery, Bellingham, Washington, 1899.
Washington State Historical Society photo.

As other packers sought to make their fortunes in this lucrative industry, they continued to study the migration habits of the salmon and used this information to build their operations where they might find the most bountiful supply of fish. This resulted in far-flung operations established for the expediency of harvesting fish, not for the comfort and convenience of the workers.

The northward trek of canneries continued. In 1878, the North Pacific Trading and Packing Company set up a small cannery at Klawock, deep in southeastern Alaska. Later that year, the Cutting Packing Company started a cannery at Sitka. In 1882, the last major salmon-producing area opened: Bristol Bay. By 1917, 118 canneries were operating in Alaska. That year, they packed more than half of the world's supply of salmon, nearly six million cases valued at $46 million.

From the very beginning of the canning industry, war created a market for canned products. The Civil War led to a sixfold increase in all U.S. canning production. Technical advances during this period helped create a permanent place for the canning industry. In the 1890s, the Spanish-American War created an important market for canned salmon. World Wars I and II also played important roles in creating stability in the salmon markets.

Consolidating Corporate Power

Where canneries were close to one another, they shared costs by closing all but one. They produced less but at higher profit. Chignik Bay canneries and then Karluk River canneries agreed to these terms as early as the 1890s.

Soon even the distance between canneries was no longer a factor in the decision to merge for profit's sake. In September 1891, Alaska canneries had a surplus of 363,000 cases. The

Alaska Packers Association (APA) was formed temporarily to dispose of the surplus. It was dissolved shortly after completing its mission, but the necessity of such an organization was very much on the minds of cannery owners. In 1892, thirty-seven Alaska salmon canneries merged to become the Alaska Packers Association. The group incorporated in 1893.

The Alaska Packers Association divided Alaska into sections, allowing only a few canneries to operate in each area, with the total profits divided up among them according to their share of stock. Out of thirty-one members in 1893, only eight were allowed to open.

Another organization, the Association of Pacific Fisheries, was formed by corporate merger in 1914. It was responsible for initiating fishery conservation legislation and researching and disseminating information relevant to fisheries.

The National Canners Association was founded in 1907. The Northwest branch began in 1917. This association consisted of nearly all companies with Alaska salmon canneries. The Salmon Terminal, Inc. was formed to handle shipping and storage of packed salmon.

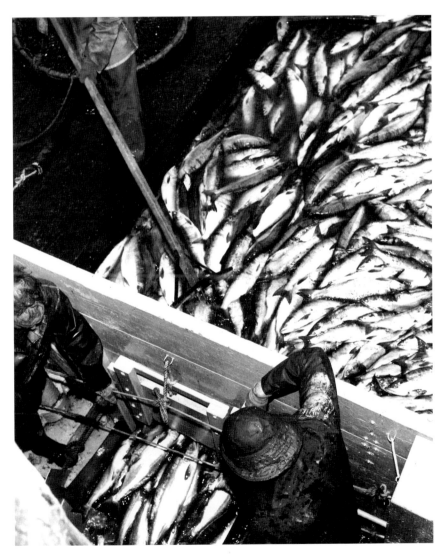

Cannery workers loading fish.
Courtesy International Examiner.

Alaska Salmon Industry, Inc., has been a dominant player. It was temporarily formed in 1934 to represent the industry in the National Recovery Administration hearings in San Francisco. From this merger came a realization that this organization was extremely helpful to individual canner companies. (APA at this time had become a subsidiary of the Del Monte Company based in California.) It was incorporated in 1940. Its initial role was to serve as the collective bargaining agent for the industry.

The Canning Line

During the salmon canning season, from early June through September, the canneries operate nearly around the clock. But during the winter, they are virtually abandoned as cold and ice descend over the water and reclaim the landscape until the following spring.

The cannery operation is a delicate balance between catching an adequate supply of fish to stoke the canning line and yet not overrun the workers who process the fish. During peak season, workers put in eighteen- and twenty-hour days, pausing only for a few hours of sleep.

As the salmon are unloaded, workers sort the fish by species. The fish are then placed in enormous bins until they are ready to be canned. They are first taken to butchering machines called "Iron Chinks," which cut off the heads, fins, and tails, open the bellies, and clean out the guts with rotating blades and brushes. The eggs are removed by hand.

As the odious name "Iron Chink" suggests, Chinese once made up the majority of workers involved in butchering the fish. Owners, eager to increase their profits, wanted to reduce their reliance on the butchers, who demanded high wages for their skilled work. Ironically, the Iron Chink—a labor-saving device conceived by Seattle inventor Edmund A. Smith, who unabashedly proclaimed that his goal was to

Iron Chink fish processor, Seattle, ca. 1909. Inventor Edmund A. Smith is at right.
Museum of History & Industry, SHS10662.

Fast-moving machinery in the canneries created workplace hazards.
Courtesy Wing Luke Museum.

create a machine so effective that the Chinese "would go home out of sheer disgust"—didn't have the intended impact.

"During its first years, the Chink replaced thousands of hand workers, but the Chink helped the salmon industry grow," writes Robert J. Browning in *Fisheries of the Pacific*. "To grow, the industry needed people and, in the end, it put more people to work all along the chain that begins with the fisherman and ends at the retail counter as much as a continent and an ocean away."

After the fish have made their way through the Iron Chink butchering machine, they continue along a conveyor belt where workers called "slimers"—each equipped with a knife, a cutting board, and a faucet of running water— clean the fish by hand.

The second phase of the process is the actual canning of the fish. Workers called "fill feeders" push the cleaned salmon into machines that cut the fish and fill empty cans with the fish. The cans are then weighed, inspected,

Cans of salmon are loaded into retorts for cooking.
Courtesy Wing Luke Museum.

Chinese workers in fish cannery, Bellingham, Washington, ca. 1900.
University of Washington Libraries, Special Collections, UW9422.

and topped off by workers called "patchers." Next, lids are placed on the cans by machine and sealed. The sealed cans are then loaded onto iron racks by workers called "can catchers." Once stacked, the cans are pushed into retorts, huge pressure-cooker chambers where the salmon is cooked. After the cans are removed and allowed to cool, they are cased up and readied for transport to market.

Part II. The Asian Labor Forces

When the spring field work comes to a grinding halt, many Filipino workers migrate north to find the one job available to them: sliming fish in the chilly fish houses of Alaska. Labor economists describe such workers as "discouraged workers." They have tried but cannot find work elsewhere, lack necessary skills, schooling, or resources, and are prevented from gaining

jobs. The "discouraged labor pool" is essential to many industries: agriculture, fruit and vegetable canneries, horticulture, and salmon canneries. Labor costs must be reduced if the producer is to provide a product with a margin of leeway for price-setting purposes.

Initially, white laborers from the East and Midwest were the "discouraged workers" who worked in the salmon canneries. They often arrived penniless. They had been lured to California by stories of prosperity and plenty. They soon found themselves still unemployed. During this era of despair, these workers turned to the unions to collectively better their lot.

Mountain of Gold

In 1872, Columbia River salmon cannery owner George Hume introduced Chinese laborers into the canned salmon industry. Convinced by his Chinese cook of their potential and reliability, he traveled to Portland, Oregon, and recruited thirty to forty Chinese. Other cannery owners also began hiring Chinese instead of white laborers who were more susceptible to unionization. At the time, Chinese were barred from joining trade unions.

This newly introduced labor force consisted of immigrants mainly from the Chinese provinces of Kwangtung and Fukien. These men, from impoverished backgrounds, were lured here by the promise of *Gum San*, or Gold Mountain. Many who left China were crowded in cramped, unsanitary ships. On some voyages, as many as one-fifth of the passengers died. Many signed on to a credit-ticket system, under which they were indentured for the next few years as payment for their passage. Their debts were then purchased by Chinese merchants already in America who contracted out their labor.

When the canneries moved north to Alaska, Chinese employees followed. In 1897, the Alaska Packers Association represented twenty-seven canneries employing 1,168 Chinese who produced 78 percent of the total Alaska canned salmon pack. Chinese dominated the canning industry's labor force for sixty years, making up an average of more than 50 percent of the cannery crews until 1933.

Under the contract system, Chinese contractors negotiated with cannery owners for services and payment in return for a set number of cases of salmon. The contractors agreed to provide laborers; the owners provided the machinery and lodging for the workers.

By the early twentieth century, the most successful and prominent of the Chinese contractors in the Northwest was Goon Dip, who became the sole supplier of workers to canneries operated by E. B. and Frank Deming in Washington and Alaska. In 1899, the Deming brothers established Pacific American Fisheries, a Bellingham-based firm that became one of the biggest processors of Pacific salmon in the world. The firm operated continuously until 1965, gradually expanding its cannery operations northward from the Columbia River and Puget Sound to British Columbia and remote areas of Alaska.

The beginning of the elimination of the Chinese from the labor pool came with the Chinese exclusion movements. When California began to face unemployment, depression, and stronger unions, criticism of "John Chinaman" grew as whites began to see the Chinese as unfair competition.

In 1882, Congress suspended immigration from China for ten years. In 1892, it extended the ban for another ten years. This diminished the labor force available to the salmon canning industry around the turn of the century. Chinese contractors who controlled the unskilled jobs then turned to Japanese immigrant laborers to fill their needs.

Japanese immigrants, like the Chinese workers before them, began travelling overseas to seek their fortune in America. Their homeland was changing from an isolated country to a country open to world trade, from an agricultural society to an industrial society. In 1899, Issei (first-generation Japanese Americans) began entering the ranks of Alaska cannery workers. By 1905, there were 1,640 Japanese cannery workers. Within seven years, they totaled 3,256.

Labor groups switched their chants of "John Chinaman Must Go" to "Japs Must Go." They were aided by numerous organizations, including the Hearst newspapers, American Legion, California State Grange, and California State Federation of Labor. The anti-Japanese campaign portrayed Japanese immigrants as greedy and refusing to become "Americanized."

With the passage of the 1924 Oriental Exclusion Act, the influx of Japanese laborers slowed, resulting in another reduction of "discouraged laborers" in the United States. Finally, the internment of Japanese during World War II eliminated Japanese labor from the Alaska salmon canneries. American industries, including the salmon canneries, sought out another labor force to draw upon.

"Little Brown Brothers"

When President William McKinley signed the Treaty of Paris in 1899, ending the Spanish-American War, the treaty left the United States in possession of the Philippines. McKinley resolved that the United States should "educate them, uplift and civilize and Christianize them and by God's grace do the very best we could by them as our fellow man for whom Christ also died."

His solution resulted in five more years of war against Filipinos who were seeking independence, costing more lives and money than the entire Spanish-American War. But his solution also eased the labor shortage in American industries. Filipinos, as wards of the U.S. government, were exempt from exclusionary legislation and could travel freely to the United States.

America was idealized as a land of opportunity. U.S. officials who ran the government of the Philippine Islands set up schools modeled after American schools: Filipinos, taught by G.I. instructors, studied out of American textbooks; they learned about George Washington, Abraham Lincoln, and Hollywood. After 1903, the Pensionado Act allowed Filipinos to study in the U.S. at the expense of the colonial government. Many of these students, called *pensionados*, returned to the Philippines with stories of the greatness of America.

Meanwhile, the U.S. occupation was taking its toll on the economy of the islands. While the Philippines exported raw resources to the United States, it imported finished U.S. products tariff-free, preventing industries in the Philippines from developing. Unemployment and overpopulation grew unchecked.

Steamship companies offered Filipinos cheap passage to America, compensating by shipping more passengers than each ship's capacity. There was overcrowding, sickness, and many deaths on these crossings. Many Filipinos arrived in California to find that jobs were scarce, except on the farms and in the canneries. They resorted to a migratory lifestyle, seeking work through Chinese and Japanese labor contractors and, increasingly, Filipino contractors. The Filipino Alaskero first appeared around 1911. By 1921, Filipinos had 957 cannery jobs. In 1927, they had 2,869. By 1928, Filipinos had become the third-largest labor force in the Alaska salmon industry after whites and Native Americans.

Increased mechanization led to reductions in jobs, but new restrictions on immigration, directed this time at Filipinos, threatened elimination of Filipinos from the canned salmon industry labor pool.

In the 1920s, the United States had begun to feel the effects of post-World War I overproduction. Factories laid off workers, and unemployment lines grew. In 1929, the Great Depression began. White workers seeking employment found themselves part of the discouraged labor pool dominated by Filipinos. Job competition intensified.

Filipinos, excluded from unions because of their race, were scapegoats for labor leaders, newspapers, and politicians running for reelection. Race riots erupted, first in Yakima and Wenatchee, Washington, and then in Exeter, Watsonville, and Los Angeles, California; and Portland, Oregon followed. In these cities, white laborers and small businessmen attempted to chase Filipinos out. Anti-Filipino groups pushed for the independence of the Philippine Islands so they could pass legislation restricting Filipino immigration.

Part III. The Contract Labor System

Under the credit-ticket system, emigrants received credit for passage to the New World. They were expected to pay back this credit through the contract labor system. The contract system was perfected in the railroad and mining industries.

Where Chinese congregated, leading merchants capitalized on their jobless countrymen, providing laborers to industries. The contract labor system came to the canning industry with the introduction of Chinese laborers. This system was essential to cannery owners due to the language barrier. The seasonal nature of cannery work also made it difficult for owners to recruit vast numbers of laborers in a short time. If they were to meet the demand for laborers, organized recruitment was necessary. Chinese who had assumed the role of contractor were given more responsibilities, until they

Chinese labor contractor Goon Dip.
Courtesy Wing Luke Museum.

were eventually in total control of hiring, supervising, feeding, and paying workers.

The racial composition of contractors shifted with the introduction of various racial workforces. Whites first exploited the Chinese, but due to the language barrier and recruitment difficulties, the Chinese merchant elite soon took their place. Chinese contractors who were successful in bidding for contracts hired the bosses or foremen, who became the subcontractors responsible for overseeing their respective canneries.

Goon Dip, a prominent Chinese businessman, subcontracted to Tsuneyoshi Kikutake, who became one of the earliest Japanese subcontractors in Seattle. Subcontractors usually operated through a Japanese hotel or boarding house, a natural gathering place for single, unemployed Japanese, usually "fresh off the boats." In 1900, there were six of these hotels. In 1905, there were more than sixty-five. In 1910, Kikuzo Uyeminami contracted directly with one of the companies. Other Japanese contractors followed suit, including Tamizo

Sakamoto, Akira Taneda, and Heitaro Obata.

With the reduction in the number of Japanese laborers and the new influx of Filipinos, it was natural that Filipinos would enter the boss and foreman ranks. Often, these men were well-educated *pensionados* who contracted directly with Alaska companies. In 1932, just before the establishment of the cannery workers labor unions, there were more than eight major Seattle Filipino contractor firms and several smaller ones hiring a total of 2,333 laborers.

Exploitative System

Experienced workers told those who had just arrived from the Philippines to do as the contractor said. They also warned, "Buy plenty to assure yourself a job. Tell them you gamble." Many were puzzled at first, but they soon understood. The contractors expected the potential recruit to buy "necessary supplies" at stores they owned. Those without money received credit toward the coming season's work.

Among the supplies were suits, shirts, suitcases, and pillows. If a laborer bought $20 in merchandise, he received a white card, which meant he had only a slight chance of getting hired. If he bought $25 of "necessary supplies," he received a red card, which meant he had a better chance of getting hired. If the laborer bought $30 or more in supplies, he was assured a job because he received a green card.

If a worker wanted a higher-paying job as a cook or a boss, the contractor saw to it that he bought between $50 and $75 of supplies. These "necessary supplies" cost two to three times as much as the same items sold on the regular market. Suits normally selling for $15 cost $45 in the contractors' stores. Often, merchandise was never delivered to the workers.

The contractor also had a solution for men without money. The storekeeper advised the worker to purchase silk shirts on credit and then go next door and pawn them. Workers bought shirts for $5 and found those shirts, never worn, depreciated to $1.50 after a twenty-five-yard walk. One desperate cannery worker bought twenty-five shirts for $125. For those shirts, he received only $37 in exchange.

Workers were forced to buy supplies such as suits to improve their chances of being hired.
Courtesy International Examiner.

A Little Book

Contract hiring was not complete until after the contractor issued the worker a little book that included a list of store expenses and hiring fees already in the minus column. The book also had a "special deduction" section. It amounted to $1 a day while the laborer waited for the boat to Alaska.

Once aboard the boats, workers felt caged in. Contractors placed wooden obstructions called "camels" between the boat and the dock to prevent anyone from jumping to the pier. If the workers cleared this obstacle, they were met by security guards hired by contractors to keep their investments "safe." Onboard, workers' quarters were cramped and segregated. On the return trip, the ship's cargo might include shipments of fish fertilizer, which cannery workers slept on. The Alaska smell stayed with them for many days.

The contractors further drained workers of money through the sale of goods on the boat. Whiskey, cigarettes, marijuana, canned goods, and citrus fruits were available at exorbitant prices. Another income source for the contractor was gambling, from which he received a cut. Once at the cannery, gambling and the sale of goods continued, but the worst exploitation was the working and living conditions. Alaskeros worked for up to six months, no less than twelve hours a day, with no days off.

Written contracts came into use in the 1920s. The contracts stipulated that all work performed after 6 P.M. was overtime. Contractors avoided paying overtime by working crews from 2 A.M. to 6 P.M.—a sixteen-hour workday with no paid overtime. Investigations in the 1930s revealed cases of bosses driving workers under the threat of bodily harm. Many bosses carried guns. Workers sick with fever sometimes worked to their deaths.

Following long hours of work, the cannery crews returned to a meal of boiled rice, dried seaweed, dried cabbage, and fish-head soup. The cannery worker's diet was whatever cost the employer the least amount of money. Contractors who maintained low food costs for their crews received kickbacks. Some contractors created demand for their goods by exhibiting food and other items for sale on the mess hall tables. Contractors encouraged cooks to salt the food heavily, causing workers to quench their thirst with something "special."

The sale of "necessary supplies," charging workers hiring fees and taking "special deductions," and skimming gambling winnings generated huge profits for contractors. On average, a six-month season ended in $140 paid to the average worker. In 1933, 555 complaints were filed by workers who had received an average of $1 to $15 for the entire season after all the contractor's deductions.

These conditions were revealed to the public and outlawed by a federal government ruling in the 1930s. Although the Supreme Court ruled President Roosevelt's National Recovery Administration unconstitutional a year later, voiding the ruling, the ruling opened the way for strong unionization drives in both Seattle and San Francisco.

Part IV. Union Ends the Cannery Contractors' Reign

After the stock market crash of 1929, many canneries closed temporarily. But job competition sharpened, resulting in increased exploitation of workers. Employers saw the oversupply of workers as their opportunity to increase profits by lowering wages.

In response, Asian workers demanded their collective bargaining rights. Chinese and Japanese in Hawaii resorted to organized sabotage, work stoppages, and strikes. In the early 1900s, eight thousand Japanese and Filipino workers walked out of the sugarcane fields, protesting low wages.

Farmers organized associations that doubled as vigilante groups and congressional lobbyists. California had its Associated Farmers, Western Growers Protective Association, and the American Institution, Inc. Thousands of vigilantes posing as legal deputies stood ready to mobilize at a moment's notice. White unions added to the barriers Asians faced. The Knights of Labor proclaimed that Asians could not become members of its order and were unfit to reside in the United States. The American Federation of Labor (AFL), under Samuel Gompers, led organized labor's move to exclude Chinese from the U.S. and supported the 1882 Chinese Exclusion Act.

In 1903, the Sugar Beet and Farm Laborers Union of Oxnard, a predominantly Japanese union, ap-pealed for AFL support. Gompers responded by demanding that the Oxnard union refuse to accept Chinese or Japanese workers under any circumstances.

Despite these barriers, Asians organized. They participated in the Industrial Workers of the World (IWW). When the Depression struck and exploitation was at its worst, Asians founded the Cannery and Allied Workers Industrial Union, Filipino Protective Union, and the Filipino Labor Union, Inc.

Initially, unionization in the Alaska canneries was rare. In 1913, the IWW established Local 283 in a Ketchikan cannery. In 1933, under the leadership of men like Virgil Duyungan, Antonio Rodrigo, C. B. Mislang, and M. Espiritu, Asian cannery workers began organizing a union in Seattle.

These early attempts at unionization met with little success at first. Filipino cannery workers were persecuted and betrayed by the

Contrary to common belief, Asian workers organized and went out on strike.
Courtesy International Examiner.

Founding members of the new Cannery Workers and Farm Laborers Union Local 18257 obtained a charter from the American Federation of Labor. Back far left: Antonio Rodrigo, treasurer. Front left: C. B. Mislang, secretary; Virgil Duyungan, president; M. Espiritu, vice-president; and Frank Alonzo.
Conrad Espe family photo. Courtesy Wing Luke Museum.

contractors. The migratory life of most cannery workers restricted year-round maintenance of union membership. Many of these men, removed from the union for long periods of time, became distrustful of union leaders.

Year-Round Membership

The early union leaders knew that membership that included all races was necessary for union efforts to succeed. In addition, salmon cannery workers who worked in the fields of California during the winter season would have to maintain membership year-round. The leaders' efforts led to an AFL charter on June 19, 1933, for the Cannery Workers and Farm Laborers Union (CWFLU) Local 18257, the first union with jurisdiction over cannery and field laborers.

The AFL, in an attempt to gain strength, joined forces with John Ayamo, a Filipino lawyer and labor activist. Ayamo traveled to San Francisco to represent the CWFLU during the National Recovery Act (NRA) code hearings investigating the salmon canning industry. The hearings resulted in the banning of the contract system because of its exploitative nature.

With this victory behind them, Local 18257 returned to a reinvigorated organizing drive. When the Maritime Union of the Pacific Coast went on strike, Local 18257 appealed for its support and received it. To gain a job in Alaska for the 1934 season, CWFLU membership was mandatory.

Meanwhile, Local 18257 negotiated a $25 raise to an unprecedented $50 a month. The membership of Local 18257 increased into the thousands. But when new members returned to

Seattle, dissension arose. Duyungan, who was elected president when the union was formed, insisted on a year-round union and demanded additional fees and union dues. Many members realized the necessity of maintaining the union and gladly paid. Others believed that the union was not much different from the contractors and refused to pay.

The union overcame the contractors' excesses during the 1934 season. When threats, blacklisting, and coercion lost their effect in intimidating workers, the contractors established the Filipino Laborers Protective Association (FLPA), which stressed cultural, social, mental, and physical development of its membership. It continued contract dispatching to the canneries. It organized in time to pull in many dissenting union members. But confusion among cannery workers led to an investigation by AFL officials, the U.S. Labor Department, and, finally, the Maritime Federation of Labor. The federation found Local 18257 and the FLPA guilty of questionable practices and immediately withdrew its support.

Immigration Quota

In 1934, Congress passed the Tydings-McDuffie Act, which set Filipino immigration quotas at fifty a year. This limited the flow of Filipino laborers to the canneries, reduced job competition, and fueled efforts to develop a stronger and more effective union that could fight to preserve cannery jobs.

In 1936, after the CWFLU gained a $5 raise for the 1935 season, the FLPA merged with the CWFLU, and their combined ranks swelled to 2,500. By this time, the union had already reduced the twelve-hour day to ten hours. With added members, Local 18257 set a goal of ending the contract system by 1937 and establishing the eight-hour day.

The contractors and employers, realizing the union was not going away, attempted one last tactic to stop the salmon canning industry from total unionization. On December 1, 1936, at the Gyokko Ken Restaurant, CWFLU officers and contractors met to discuss the coming season. There, Beseda Patron, a nephew of a

CWFLU Local 18257 officials and members at Fifth Avenue and Main Street headquarters in the International District on Labor Day, September 7, 1936.
Conrad Espe family photo. Courtesy Wing Luke Museum.

contractor, shot Local 18257 president Virgil Duyungan and secretary Aurelio Simon. Before this attack, Duyungan and his family had received threats. Duyungan carried a gun and returned fire before he died, killing Patron.

Thousands of maritime workers attended Duyungan's funeral. The march spanned six blocks of downtown Seattle, demonstrating the strength of workers in unity. Inspired, CWFLU Local 18257 ended the contractors' reign in the salmon canning industry by the 1937 season.

Part V. A Militant Union Copes with Disruptive Tactics

After Duyungan's death, Conrad Espe took the lead role in the union. Although the union ended the contract hiring system, all was not well. Under the leadership of Duyungan and Espe, the CWFLU had attempted to organize winter field workers. Farm division organizers unionized agricultural workers in Yakima, Kent, Everett, and the White River area. In

Kent, organizers were met by vigilante groups led by the town's mayor. In Yakima, they were imprisoned by police-led vigilantes.

By the early 1930s, the AFL was divided between the traditional craft unionists and the more radical-minded industrial trade workers. United Mine Workers president John L. Lewis advocated separation of the industrial trade line from the AFL in 1932, the faction that split and formed the Congress of Industrial Organizations (CIO). By the late 1930s, AFL Local 18257 members considered affiliating with the CIO.

The AFL leadership, to dissuade unions breaking away to join the CIO, initiated divisive tactics. In 1937, AFL organizer Leo Flynn proposed the division of all cannery unions into racially autonomous union affiliates. He chartered CIarence T. Arai's Local 20454, a Japanese group, and appealed to the other races to follow suit. He also announced that these unions would be governed by a board headed by Conrad Espe.

These AFL tactics increased the number of cannery workers who wished to reaffiliate with the CIO. In the winter of 1937, planning

Cannery workers delegation in the May Day parade, 1937.
Courtesy International Examiner.

began in earnest for the establishment of an international of cannery, packinghouse, and field workers under the CIO.

In the salmon canning industry, the AFL demanded that employers recognize only Arai's Local 20454 during the 1937 negotiations. Local 18257 responded with a restraining order and immediately negotiated for an eight-hour day, closed union shop, and wage increases. The Japanese union picketed Local 18257 on May Day, 1937, in an attempt to keep its workers from going north. Local 18257 workers marched 1,200 strong through Local 20454's picket line. This delegation later marched in the May Day parade, the largest unit in the whole demonstration.

The AFL suspended Local 18257 for disregarding the picket lines and urged the Seattle Central Labor Council (SCLC) to deny support. Both the labor council and the Maritime Federation of Labor defended the CWFLU and commended its members for their militant stand.

In July 1937, Local 18257 delegates returned from the CIO congress in Denver. The delegates reported the formation of the United Cannery, Agricultural, Packing and Allied Workers of America (UCAPAWA). This new international represented farm, cannery, packinghouse, and dairy farm workers. The delegates urged the CWFLU to reaffiliate. On November 4, 1937, the union members voted to reaffiliate with the CIO. Local 18257-AFL became UCAPAWA Local 7-CIO.

UCAPAWA's ranks swelled to 124,750 nationally by December 1938. Among its most militant members were those in the Alaska cannery workers unions: Local 7 in Seattle, Local 5 in San Francisco, and Local 226 in Portland. Between these three locals, 6,000 cannery workers provided half the funds necessary to create UCAPAWA.

Intimidation and Disruption

After Local 18257's reaffiliation with the CIO, the AFL and the industry intimidated and disrupted the union. The AFL issued the old charter of Local 18257 to John Ayamo and other members who opposed the reaffiliation. Called the "Defeated Candidates Party" by

NLRB election to determine exclusive bargaining representation, May 1938.
Courtesy Wing Luke Museum.

Local 7 members, it immediately began a red-baiting campaign, calling Conrad Espe and his cohorts the "Communist Comics."

The industry followed suit, announcing through Canned Salmon Industry, Inc. (CSI), that it would deal only with AFL unions. Former labor contractors joined in the attack by offering free meals in their restaurants to any who surrendered their CIO books. Local 7-CIO responded by filing a complaint of unfair labor practices with the National Labor Relations Board (NLRB).

Disruptive tactics increased. The AFL collaborated with immigration authorities and the Federal Bureau of Investigation. Many Local 7 members were arrested under bogus charges. Local 7 immediately applied for an NLRB consent audit that would reaffirm its representation of cannery workers.

The company foremen met on April 1, 1938. At the meeting, each foreman received the names of twenty crew members they were to coerce into voting for Local 18257 by threatening the crew members with the loss of their jobs. The NLRB stepped in after Local 7 leadership again filed claims against the industry for unfair labor practices. Local 7 won the consent audit with 1,597 votes, Local 18257 got 685 votes, and there were 504 neutral votes.

A New Election

The NLRB set the date for a new election. The industry and the AFL again intimidated cannery workers. Casimiro A. Abella, the secretary of Local 7, was arrested, but no charges were filed. Other union members were harassed on the streets, and their hotel rooms were searched.

The mayor of Seattle, having close ties with the industry, pushed the police chief to intimidate Local 7. He informed the NLRB that the local police would provide a riot team at the election site. The NLRB asked the U.S. marshal to intervene. The U.S. marshal informed the police chief that supervision of the election would be done by his office.

Both unions competed fiercely for votes. On election day, numerous fights broke out. Election supervisors created two lines, one for Local 18257 and the other for Local 7. Following the four-day election, union members crowded around the election site waiting for the results. Local 7 won, 1,560 to 1,307.

The AFL refused to sanction the election and protested to the NLRB. On May 10, 1938, Local 18257 attempted to dispatch its workers, but the CIO picketed the Alaska transportation docks. With the support of the Maritime Federation of the Pacific, no AFL workers were dispatched to Alaska. On May 11, Local 7 dispatched its crews through an AFL picket line.

Local 7 Negotiates

With this victory under its belt, Local 7-CIO entered negotiations with the industry. After the election, Canned Salmon Industry formally recognized the CIO, and both AFL unions died out. The cannery workers also

THE SEATTLE DAILY TIMES

UNIONS, SALMON CANNERS SIGN AGREEMENT

Representatives of the Canned Salmon Industry and of the locals of the United Cannery, Agricultural, Packing & Allied Workers of America, a Congress of Industrial Organization, yesterday afternoon signed an agreement covering wages for more than 7,000 Pacific Coast cannery workers for 1939. Gathered around a conference table in the Exchange Building to sign the pact or witness its execution were the following: Seated, left to right—I. R. Cabatit, of Local No. 7 of the union; Conrad Espe, international vice president; E. M. Breman, of the P. E. Harris Company; George Downer, United States Department of Labor con-ciliator; Capt. F. Swensson, of Libby, McNeill & Libby, and H. B. Frielⁱ vice president and general manager, Nakat Packing Corporatioⁱ Standing, left to right—I. I. Josue, Seattle, Local No. 7; Mrs. Marguerit Hanson, Ketchikan, Local No. 237; E. A. Mangaoang, Portland, Locⁱ No. 226; George W. Woolf, San Francisco, president of Local No. 5 A. I. Ellsworth, executive secretary, Canned Salmon Industry; Ernest ⁱ Marsh, Department of Labor conciliator; Harold C. Jones, Petersbur Local No. 222; John E. O'Connor, Department of Labor conciliatoⁱ Eugene V. Dennett, secretary of the Washington State Council, Congres of Industrial Organization, and V. O. Navea, Local No. 7.

Courtesy Wing Luke Museum.

accepted a 14 percent wage cut. The industry made special appeals to both the union and the government, stressing drastic reductions in profits in previous years.

In December 1938, John Ayamo received a new AFL charter to form the Alaska Fish Cannery Workers Union of the Pacific under the jurisdiction of the Seafarers International Union. His union recruited 190 men, who worked for six companies.

Irineo R. Cabatit was president of Local 7-CIO following Duyungan's death and the union-busting attacks by the industry and the ousted contractors. Trinidad Rojo became president in 1939. The new leadership discovered that officers under Cabatit had sold membership cards, charged personal purchases on union accounts, and neglected their work. The union was on the verge of bankruptcy, with $13,000 in debt.

Rojo drew up a strict budget, cut the number of employees by half, and implemented a system of expenditure authorization. The wages of officers dropped from $35 and $20 a week to $7 and $5. Fund-raisers were held to support the floundering union. The union then negotiated a 33 percent increase in wages. Overtime pay was raised to sixty cents an hour. In addition, the union gained the right to appoint all foremen. During Rojo's term, World War II broke out. Rojo declined the nomination for the presidency in 1940. His successor was Vicente O. Navea.

Part VI. Cannery Workers Union, World War II, and the McCarthy Era

In 1940, the United States government instituted a fish conservation program, reducing salmon packs by 50 percent. This meant the loss of a significant number of jobs. The companies again asked for a wage cut, but Local 7-CIO resisted this demand, and wage rates remained as they were under the 1939 contract.

Shortly after the United States entered World War II, half the union's militant leaders were drafted. Other union members considered it hopeless to continue to fight for higher wages and better conditions. Many workers signed up for military service.

To ensure a united, nationwide effort, the U.S. government established the War Production Board, which would oversee allocation of fuel and other resources. The government also implemented wage freezes, a no-strike clause, and travel restrictions.

Subsequently, Local 7-CIO developed new functions. It began helping alien workers complete registration cards and Alaska travel permits. The union became known as an international consulate. It also began policing rental facilities in Seattle's Chinatown, forcing landlords to obey rent-control laws.

The government set up an adjustment board, consisting of three company and three union officials, to handle complaints by workers. Cannery workers showed their patriotism by accepting no wage increase in 1943 and only a 7 percent increase in 1945.

The Move to Seattle

During the late 1930s and through World War II, many cannery companies moved their main offices from San Francisco and Portland to Seattle, to cut down on transportation costs to Alaska.

Locals 5 and 226 originally formed as members of the United Cannery, Agricultural, Packing and Allied Workers of America. During negotiations, the locals merged temporarily. In 1940, the International suggested that this temporary merger become permanent.

When the industry moved its main offices to Seattle, it also consolidated as a permanent corporation, the Alaska Salmon Industry, Inc., originally formed during the National Recovery Act hearings in 1934. It functioned as the principal party in contract negotiations.

In 1943, the last of the big cannery companies moved to Seattle, leaving the San Francisco and Portland offices virtually inactive. Locals 5 and 226 protested amalgamation, arguing that their members would lose seniority

Returning World War II veterans were anxious to continue the fight for decent wages through their union. *Courtesy* International Examiner.

and face potential discrimination in dispatching. The San Francisco local consisted of many Mexicans, blacks, and some Chinese. The two locals feared that since the foremen would be chosen by a vote of the membership, Local 7 would be able to reelect its foremen.

Finally, on July 12, 1943, the three locals merged, with stipulations added to appease the Portland and San Francisco locals. Local 7 took strides to increase its membership. The unions took on anti-Fascist and anti-Communist sentiments stemming from their desire to align with U.S. positions during the War.

When Local 7 held its biannual election in October 1944, it resolved that: "No strike breakers or an expelled member of a *bona fide* organization; nor those holding membership in an organization dual to that of the union; and others who tend to work against the interest of the association, shall be admitted to membership."

Rebirth of Dualism

Internal divisions erupted in a rebirth of dualism. Members of the Caballeros de Dimas Alang, a Filipino fraternal organization founded in 1906 to support independence for the Philippines, gained control of the union. In 1945, when President Casimiro A. Abella appointed his friends from the same township in the Philippines to union positions, members became disgruntled with the blatant cronyism and called for change.

During the 1946 election, the Dimas Alang ran a full slate of candidates for union leadership positions, except for the president's position, which they reserved for Prudencio Mori. Mori had led a successful strike of resident cannery workers in Ketchikan in 1939. He served as vice president from 1942 to 1943 and as secretary from 1943 to 1945.

The slate easily won. Max Gonzales, a Di-

Chris Mensalvas, Sr., ca. 1930s.
Chris Mensalvas, Jr. collection.

mas Alang member, became vice president. Through intimidation, he controlled most of the executive board. In 1944, he appointed 90 percent of all foremen from among Dimas Alang members and then expected Mori to accede to his wishes.

Conflict between Mori and Gonzales came to a head at the January 1947 Food, Tobacco, Agricultural and Allied Workers of America (FTA) convention in Philadelphia. There, the Local 7 delegation was denied seats because Local 7 owed the International back dues in unemployment fees.

The International officials and Local 7 agreed that the local would pay half the dues owed because of the seasonal nature of cannery work. The International agreed that the delegation could be seated, but with only 50 percent of its convention votes.

Local 7 delegates, minus Mori, accepted this agreement. Their interest was focused on opposition to a proposed resolution to exclude foremen and supervisory employees from holding major offices in the locals and to limit the numbers of foremen on executive boards. Local 7 was intent on countering this amendment because its officers were predominantly company foremen, but in the end, its effort was unsuccessful.

Where Is Our Union?

In June 1946, the *SS Santa Cruz* steamed out of Seattle with 1,200 cannery workers. They hadn't been aboard long, but they were already mad. Below deck, men squeezed into cramped bunks, exhausted from carrying their blankets, suitcases, and sea bags three decks below. The bunks, the food, and the lavatories were filthy and inadequate.

They wondered why their union had allowed these problems to persist. After thirteen years, they still didn't have a union strong enough to change these intolerable conditions. These men had returned from a war in which they proved their allegiance, a war that had forced the United States to give them citizenship. They demanded treatment as equals. They held a meeting aboard ship and elected committees to lead their fight for better treatment and working conditions.

The determination to strengthen union activism stayed with the workers throughout the season. On the way back from the canneries aboard the *SS Young America*, more union members spoke up. At a meeting, they voted to establish themselves as the Rank-and-File Committee, to push for change in the union from the bottom up. They elected Chris Mensalvas, Leo Lorenzo, and Mario Hermosa to lead the way.

Upon arrival in Seattle, the steering committee presented the demands of the Rank-and-File Committee to the union leadership. It soon became apparent the officials were not going to do any more than they had done in past years. The Rank-and-File Committee prepared for the upcoming fight.

"Shut Up"

On February 9, 1947, representatives returning from the Philadelphia convention gave their report. The Rank-and-File Committee was ready. During the report, Matias Lagunilla demanded that Max Gonzales explain why he had not notified President Mori of the delegation's opposition to the resolution banning foremen from union leadership proposed by Local 7 delegates.

Gonzales told Lagunilla, "Shut up." Lagunilla responded, "Shut up yourself." Gonzales pulled a gun, ran toward Lagunilla, and fired. Lagunilla ran for cover, and the shot missed. Gonzales was convicted of assault in civil court. At a March 24, 1947, executive board meeting, Lagunilla presented charges against Gonzales, but the board refused to expel Gonzales, ruling that he had acted in self-defense.

Upon appeal to the International executive board, Gonzales was formally expelled. Local 7, however, ignored the International's decision, and Gonzales continued to hold office and participate in Local 7 affairs. Local 7 leaders then requested that the International grant an exemption from the rule barring foremen from leadership that had passed at the Philadelphia convention. The International ruled that the foremen could serve out their terms but must not run for reelection. On June 11, 1947, Local 7's executive board rejected the International's decision. A week later, Gonzales proposed that the executive board dissolve and form another union independent of the FTA, retaining the old leadership.

On June 20, 1947, the International sent John Tisa to investigate Local 7, with instructions to gain the help of Mori. Tisa and Mori's report to the International pointed to "acts of misconduct made possible by illegally dispensing membership books and jobs, by misuse of union funds, and by outright terrorism, intimidation and threats, of which the attempt to shoot a union member in a regular union meeting is an outstanding example."

They recommended that the International act immediately to prevent further corruption. The International suspended all officers of Local 7 and set up an administrative board with Trinidad Rojo as president, Mori as secretary, and Ernesto Mangaoang as business agent.

Seafood Workers Union

The administrative officers appointed by the International easily won the election on September 24, 1947. The ousted officers immediately formed the Seafood Workers Union (SFWU). That winter, the SFWU launched a membership campaign. During one week, 600 men were signed into their union in California. Local 7 had 3,500 members. Local 7 officials believed this membership drive was funded by the Alaska Salmon Industry, Inc. SFWU officials said, however, that the union was funded by contributions from its members.

In October 1947, Alaska Salmon Industry,

(From left) Casimiro A. Abella, Matias J. Lagunilla, Trinidad A. Rojo, and Ernesto Mangaoang. 1952 ILWU Yearbook. *IBU, Region 37 collection.*

Negotiations, 1952. Seated (left to right): Gene Navarro, Dispatcher; Lazaro Soria, Patrolman; Johnny Lucero, Negotiations Committee; Ernesto Mangaoang, Business Agent; Rudy M. Rodriguez, Executive Board; George A. Valdez, Vice President and Educational and Publicity Director. Standing (left to right): Trinidad A. Rojo, Executive Board; Pantaleon Cabuena, Executive Board; Chris D. Mensalvas, President; Ted Daddeo, Trustee; Matias J. Lagunilla, Secretary.
1952 ILWU Yearbook. *IBU, Region 37 collection.*

Inc., and the Seafood Workers Union filed for a representation election. The petition to the National Labor Relations Board said the International Food, Tobacco, Agricultural and Allied Workers of America and Local 7 officials had not signed the non-Communist affidavits required under the Taft-Hartley Act. The SFWU distributed leaflets titled "Revealing the Communist Leaning of Local 7 and the FTA Are Exposed." They filed lawsuits and petitions. Local 7 responded by countersuing.

In the courts, the SFWU demanded that Local 7 be dissolved. The courts ordered Local 7 to turn over its books to the SFWU for investigation. Local 7 officials refused, instead turning them over to Matias Lagunilla, head of the Local 7 Defense Committee. All Local 7 officials were fined for contempt. On April 2, 1948, Lagunilla was jailed. After filing writs of habeas corpus, he was released. Rojo later resigned from the presidency, saying he did not

want to become embroiled in a contempt suit. Ray A. Cabanilla took over as president.

Once the books were examined by the courts, the case was withdrawn. Meanwhile, the ASI withheld the dues taken out during the 1948 season. A total of $61,817 in membership dues was not turned over to Local 7 coffers. The courts ruled that the money should go to Local 7. A year and a half later, in December 1948, the money was finally turned over to Local 7 officials. After creditors, back wages, lawyers, and court fees were paid, only $3,000 remained.

Representation Election

A representation election, petitioned for by the SFWU, was scheduled for June 1948. The NLRB ruled that Local 7 was a "non-compliance union" but also ruled that the SFWU was a company union. Due to this complication, the industry drafted a contract, and Local 7 dispatched its workers without signing it. Under the terms of this agreement, workers gained first-class passage rather than steerage. But the standby pay of $67.50 was eliminated.

Following the NLRB ruling, the SFWU merged with the Alaska Fish Cannery Workers Union–Seafarers International Union, which was formed during the 1938 dual union period and still had 190 members. The officials of this new union, the Alaska Fish Cannery Workers Union (AFCWU), were John Ayamo, president; Cornelio Briones, business agent; and Victor Velasco, secretary-treasurer.

Once again, a petition for representation elections was filed with the NLRB. In the hearing, the NLRB denied representation to Local 7, ruling that the FTA-lnternational had not filed non-Communist affidavits. Also, because the 1948 contract was never officially signed, Local 7 held no contractual agreement giving it jurisdiction over the 3,500 members of Local 7. The NLRB found that Local 7's representation of its members was in question and set an election for April 1949. The ASI then offered two identical contracts, one to Local 7 and one to AFCWU. There were no wage increases, and the industry reinserted the miscellaneous work clause. Under the contract, the industry had the right to choose foremen and had total control over the selection of workers. The new contract also removed company store price restraints.

The AFCWU immediately signed the agreement, but Local 7 refused to agree to the conditions. The next day, the *Seattle Post-Intelligencer* falsely reported that the industry had awarded AFCWU sole representation of cannery workers. AFCWU followed up with a leaflet announcing victory over Local 7. Agents went up and down the West Coast to get workers to sign up for jobs with the AFCWU. Workers signed up with AFCWU to ensure keeping their jobs in Alaska. Some became members of both unions.

Meanwhile, ASI negotiations with Local 7 stalled. More men went over to the AFL union. On May 24, 1949, Local 7 signed out of fear of losing more members. The preliminary

agreement did not include any wage increases.

With the election hotly contested, both sides lobbied heavily for votes. Local 7 said AFCWU was a company union, that it was racist, anti-Oriental and anti-Negro. Local 7 said AFCWU members had the reputation of being scabs and anti-union. AFCWU said Local 7 was Communist-dominated and subversive to the American system.

Attack on the Union

Dual unionism caused havoc for cannery workers during the 1949 election. As in the 1938 election when immigration officers arrested union leaders, immigration officers again walked into the Local 7 headquarters and arrested business agent Ernesto Mangaoang and charged him with being a member of the Communist Party who advocated the overthrow of the government by force or violence. Local 7 immediately created a defense fund. Chris Mensalvas, president of Local 7, was also arrested. Mori was twice questioned by immigration agents.

Pickets surrounded the immigration office. One hundred sixty cannery workers demanded Mangaoang's release. They chanted, "We want Ernie" and "You can't scare me; I'm sticking to the union." Later that day, the $5,000 bail was raised and Mangaoang was released.

Due to the unfavorable image the FTA-lnternational had gained, it was finally expelled from the National CIO. Following this, many Local 7 officers resigned for fear of being arrested as Communists. Many of these officers and many more cannery workers merged to form Local 77, United Packinghouse Workers of America (UPWA)-CIO, with Vicente O. Navea as president.

Meanwhile, on March 26, 1950, Local 7 reaffiliated with the International Longshoremen's and Warehousemen's Union (ILWU) and became known as Local 7-C, ILWU. An NLRB election was set to establish who would then have collective bargaining rights with the Alaska Salmon Industry.

Local 7-C waged a battle against Local 77 and the Alaska Fish Cannery Workers Union.

Local 7-C, ILWU won the election. Local 7-C immediately filed for a union shop election. The election this time was between a united cannery workers union and the Alaska Salmon Industry. Local 7-C won and was awarded a four-year contract. Local 7-C became Local 37 of the ILWU.

Part VII. The Next Alaska Cannery Workers

In the 1970s, the existence of the Filipino crews is in jeopardy. Work in the salmon industry is increasingly scarce. For the past forty years, five thousand to six thousand Filipino workers have been employed, helping develop the Alaska salmon canning industry into one of the largest and most profitable industries in Alaska. By 1977, Filipino cannery workers numbered no more than five hundred.

The industry is curtailing production, and the majority of the blame can be placed on the declining supply of salmon. But what explains the trend to hire white, female, college-age workers and Native Americans? In the past, cannery crews consisted primarily of Asians, but crews are now divided between college-age females, Native Americans, and Filipinos.

These female workers are from the lower forty-eight states, as are the Filipino workers. They are members of Local 37, ILWU. The Native Americans are residents of Alaska and belong to their respective resident cannery workers union. The majority of these people have no cannery work experience.

The Filipino cannery crews changed little before 1965. These men were the same Filipino immigrants who came seeking the American Dream, the men who fought the contractors, started the union, and then fought the exploitative fishing companies. Manongs embrace "bahala na," or "happen what may." They will live the rest of their lives in the society that denied them employment, freedom to marry, or even the dignity to walk the streets without being assaulted or called "monkeys."

They have earned the peace they seek, but the American-born generation who entered the salmon canning labor force in the early 1960s now make up over half of the crews. This generation has found many of the same unjust conditions that the *manongs* fought to change for more than a half a century.

These young men were raised in what the *manongs* pictured as their American Dream: a good education, a home, a car, a wife and family. The contradictions of cannery life were not lost on young Filipino Americans. Many made their high school honor rolls, excelled in athletics, and even attained college degrees. It was impossible for them to accept segregated living quarters, unsanitary mess halls, and unsafe working conditions, so they complained and many rebelled.

"Good" Crews

To explain the change in the labor force from Filipinos to white females and Native Americans, one must remember the historic hiring practices of the industry. When one group of workers became dissatisfied and complained about wages or living and working conditions, a new force was introduced, usually consisting of the largest, least organized workforce available at the time.

"Good" crews complain little and accept low wages. The "good" crews of tomorrow seem to be young, college-age females and Native Americans.

According to canners, the lack of cannery facility improvements is due to losses of revenue since the government banned fish traps. Once fish traps were illegal, it became necessary to build large fishing fleets in order to ensure an adequate supply of raw salmon. Much of the profit that should have gone into cannery modernization went into building boats and luring fishermen away from other employers, enabling canners to maintain an adequate fish supply. Meanwhile, the workers were ignored.

Once again, forces are lining up for a confrontation between canneries and the efforts of unions to organize labor. Alaska residents, complaining of the lack of jobs, are unionizing to protect their interests, Native Americans are

Courtesy International Examiner.

joining resident workers unions, and nonresident Filipinos from the lower forty-eight are demanding their fair share of jobs.

This confrontation may be averted with the availability of new jobs from the bottom-fishing fisheries. However, these jobs become available only if the company has enough profit to finance these endeavors. Meanwhile, the industry continues to cut costs at the expense of safe, sanitary, and modern working and living conditions. The Alaska salmon industry once again benefits from competition between workers, as they did during the depression of the 1800s, World War I, the Great Depression, and post–World War II recessions. This competition will eventually eliminate the labor force that is unwilling to put up with poor working conditions and low wages.

The unanswered question is: Who will be the "good" crews of the future?

REFERENCES

Books and Articles

Andrews, Ralph W., and A. K. Larssen. *Fish and Ships*. Seattle: Superior Publishing Co., 1959.

"Appeals Court Upholds Baruso Murder Conviction." *Seattle Post-Intelligencer*, 27 November 1993.

Bacho, Peter. *Alaskeros: A Documentary Exhibit on Pioneer Filipino Cannery Workers*. Seattle: Pioneer Alaskero Project, 1990.

———. "Chris Mensalvas: The Meaning of a Life Well Lived." *International Examiner* (Seattle), 15 September 1982.

Birkland, Dave. "Ex-union Chief Charged in Slayings: Baruso Long Considered Suspect In 1981 Killings of Two Activists." *Seattle Times*, 6 September 1990.

Browning, Robert J. *Fisheries of the North Pacific: History, Species, Gear and Processes*. Anchorage: Alaska Northwest Publishing Co., 1974.

"Cannery Union Ousts Secretary-Treasurer." *International Examiner* (Seattle), October 1979.

"Cannery Workers Await Court Action on Discrimination Suit." *International Examiner* (Seattle), October 1977.

"Cannery Workers Exhibit on Display." *International Examiner* (Seattle), July 1977.

"Cannery Workers' Victory: Local 37 Elections." *International Examiner* (Seattle), October 1980.

Chew, Ron. "Alaska Cannery Workers Await Court Ruling on Historic Discrimination Suit." *International Examiner* (Seattle), November 1976.

———. "Cannery Workers Awaiting Court Decision." *International Examiner* (Seattle), May 1976.

———. "Gene Viernes: The Alaska Experience." *International Examiner* (Seattle), June 1981.

———. "Local Cannery Union Moves from Its Deteriorating Building." *International Examiner* (Seattle), 5 March 1986.

———. "Memorable Years at the International Examiner; The Examiner Takes a Final Look Back at 30 Years of History." *International Examiner* (Seattle), 1 December 2004.

———. "Minority Cannery Workers Eligible for Discrimination Money." *International Examiner* (Seattle), January 1978.

Chin, Doug. "Fighting for Worker's Rights: Northwest Labor and Employment Law Offices (LELO)." *International Examiner* (Seattle), 17 April 2002.

———. *Seattle's International District: The Making of a Pan-Asian American Community*. Seattle: International Examiner Press, 2001.

Chin, Sue. "Baruso Will Be Tried on Voter Fraud."
International Examiner (Seattle), 12 August 1981.

———. "Jury Convicts Ramil and Guloy of Murder." *International Examiner* (Seattle), 7 October 1981.

———. "Murder Trial Enters Fifth Week." *International Examiner* (Seattle), 11 September 1981.

———. "Police Investigate Murder of Union Leaders." *International Examiner* (Seattle), 16 July 1981.

———. "Union President Arrested and Released." *International Examiner* (Seattle), 20 July 1981.

"Chris Mensalvas Dies from Apartment Fire." *International Examiner* (Seattle), April 1978.

"Clinton against Exemption for Wards Cove." *Seattle Times*, 3 March 1993.

"Construction Civil Rights Leader Dies at Age 63." *Vancouver Columbian*, 21 June 2003.

"Dictado Scheduled to Go on Trial November 30." *International Examiner* (Seattle), November 1981.

Domingo, Cindy. "Separate and Unequal: The Historic Wards Cove Discrimination Case." *Filipinas*, October 2001.

Eskenazi, Stuart. "Wards Cove Lawsuit Back in Court Again." *Seattle Times*, 6 August 2000.

Friday, Chris. *Organizing Asian American Labor: The Pacific Coast Canned-Salmon Industry, 1870–1942*. Philadelphia: Temple University Press, 1994.

Guillen, Tomas. "Hundreds Mourn Slain Union Official." *Seattle Times*, 4 June 1981.

Guillen, Tomas, and Dave Birkland. "Union Aide Slain, 2nd Hurt; Link to Earlier Killing Probed." *Seattle Times*, 2 June 1981.

"Half of Fish Consumed Globally Is Now Raised on Farms." *Science Daily*, 8 September 2009, at http://www.sciencedaily.com/releases/2009/09/090907162320.htm (accessed 22 July 2011).

Hopkins, Jack, "Baruso Finally Faces Trial in 1981 Union Murders; His Lawyer Says the Defendant May Testify." *Seattle Post-Intelligencer*, 11 February 1991.

———. "Baruso Sentenced to Life in Prison." *Seattle Post-Intelligencer*, 20 April 1991.

———. "Deliberations to Continue in Aggravated Murder Trial." *Seattle Post-Intelligencer*, 5 March 1991.

———. "Doctor Denies He Ever Met Baruso; Charges of Payoff Money in Cannery Killings Disputed." *Seattle Post-Intelligencer*, 28 February 1991.

———. "Inmates Take the Fifth on Slayings." *Seattle Post-Intelligencer*, 20 February 1991.

———. "Marcos Link to Slayings Supported; Official Says Foes Intimidated." *Seattle Post-Intelligencer*, 26 February 1991.

"ILWU Local Celebrates International Workers Day." *International Examiner* (Seattle), May 1978.

"Imelda Marcos Ordered to Pay $2 Million in Unionists' Deaths." *Washington Post*, 21 May 1991.

Iritani, Evelyn. "Hot Potato Cannery Suit Bounces from Courts to Congress." *Seattle Post-Intelligencer*, 25 May 1992.

Iwamoto, Gary. "From I.D. Neighborhood Paper to Asian American Community Voice." *International Examiner* (Seattle), 14 June 1994.

Jacobi, Wayne. "Tears and Vows at Funeral for Murdered Union Officers." *Seattle Post-Intelligencer*, 4 June 1981.

"Judge OKs Settlement of Suit against Marcos." *Los Angeles Times*, 25 May 1991.

"Judge to Rule in Favor of Cannery Workers." *International Examiner* (Seattle), April 1977.

Jue, Willard "Goon Dip: Entrepreneur, Diplomat and Community Leader." In *The Annals of the Chinese Historical Society of the Pacific Northwest*. Bellingham, Wash.: Center for East Asian Studies, 1984.

"Jury Selection Begins in Trial of Ex-cannery Union Chief." *Seattle Post-Intelligencer*, 13 February 1991.

Koslosky, Nancy Ordona, and Julia Laranang. "Filipino Migrant Labor: To the Farms and to the Canneries." *International Examiner* (Seattle), November 1976.

"Labor Organizer Tyree Scott Passes Away at Age 63." *International Examiner* (Seattle), 2 July 2003.

Laranang, Julia. "Cannery Union Votes to Recall Baruso." *International Examiner* (Seattle), 16 December 1981.

———. "Filipino Community Activist Sues Police Department." *International Examiner* (Seattle), July 1977.

———. "Silme Domingo: A Revolutionary, a Friend." *International Examiner* (Seattle), June 1981.

Lin, Melissa. "The Long Journey to Justice: A History of the Wards Cove Case." *International Examiner* (Seattle), 1 August 2000.

Luna, Deni. "Cindy Domingo's Commitment to the Community Is Unswerving in the Face of Adversity." *Northwest Asian Weekly* (Seattle), 5 January 1996.

"Marcos Allies Found Liable in '81 Killings." *Washington Post*, 14 January 1981.

"Marcos Said to Admit Spying on U.S. Foes." *Los Angeles Times*, 16 July 1986.

"Marcos to Stand Trial for Domingo and Viernes Murders." *The Dispatcher* (San Francisco), 15 June 1989.

"Marcoses Held Civilly Liable in Two Murders." *Washington Post*, 16 December 1989.

Masson, Jack K., and Donald L. Guimary. "Pilipinos and Unionization of the Alaskan Canned Salmon Industry." *Amerasia Journal* 8, no. 2 (Fall–Winter 1981).

Murkowski, Frank H. "Wards Cove: Some Facts Wrong in Editorial about Alaska Cannery Lawsuit." *Seattle Times*, 9 May 1992.

Ocampo, Ben. "Crowds Pack Memorial Services." *Ang Katipunan* (Oakland, Calif.), 1 July 1981.

———. "In Slayings." *Ang Katipunan* (Oakland, Calif.), 1 August 1981.

"Old Cannery Reborn as Tourist Attraction." *USA Today*, 20 September 2004.

"Oops! Bill May Have Lost Its Ward's Cove Exemption." *Seattle Times*, 1 November 1991.

Sahagun, Louis. "Ex-union Chief Guilty in Murder Crime: A Prominent Filipino-American Is Convicted of Arranging the Death of a Seattle Labor Reformer Who Opposed Ferdinand Marcos." *Los Angeles Times*, 9 March 1991.

Santos, Bob. *Hum Bows, Not Hot Dogs!: Memoirs of a Savvy Asian American Activist*. Seattle: International Examiner Press, 2002.

———. "Our Very Good Friends Gene and Silme." *International Examiner* (Seattle), June 1981.

"Seattle Lawyer Fights for the 'Little Guy.'" *Seattle Post-Intelligencer*, 15 July 2006.

Serrano, Barbara A. "Baruso Guilty of One Murder: Former Union Leader's Term Means He Must Serve Life without Parole." *Seattle Times*, 1 March 1991.

Shimabukuro, Robert. "Activist's Strategizing Reaped Benefits for Others." *International Examiner* (Seattle), 6 June 1995.

Smith, Carlton, and Amy Kuebelbeck. "A Family's Long Search for Justice." *Seattle Times*, 7 September 1990.

Stamets, John. "The Cannery Murders." *The Weekly* (Seattle), 4 August 1982.

Sunde, Scott, and Jack Hopkins. "Baruso Found Guilty; Jury Convicts Him of One Union Killing, Clears Him of Another." *Seattle Post-Intelligencer*, 9 March 1991.

"'Tony' Baruso, Former Union President Convicted of Murder, Dies in Prison." *Seattle Times*, 14 November 2008.

"Two Charged with Aggravated Murder." *Ang Katipunan* (Oakland, Calif.), 1 July 1981.

Viernes, Gene. "Cannery Workers Lawsuit: Who's to Gain?" *International Examiner* (Seattle), May 1979.

———. "Chris Mensalvas: Daring to Dream." *International Examiner* (Seattle), May 1978.

———. "NEFCO Goes Under." *International Examiner* (Seattle), May 1980.

———. "Part 1: Here's How They Created the Salmon Canning Industry." *International Examiner* (Seattle), February 1977.

———. "Part 2: Sliming and Butchering in the Alaska Canneries." *International Examiner* (Seattle), March 1977.

———. "Part 3: The Contract Labor System in the Canneries." *International Examiner* (Seattle), April 1977.

———. "Part 4: Union Ends Reign of Cannery Contractors." *International Examiner* (Seattle), May 1977.

———. "Part 5: A Militant Union Copes with Disruptive Tactics." *International Examiner* (Seattle), May 1977.

———. "Part 6: Cannery Workers' Union Emerges from the War Years and McCarthy Era." *International Examiner* (Seattle), June 1977.

———. "Part 7: Who Will Be the Alaska Cannery Workers of the Future?" *International Examiner* (Seattle), August 1977.

———. "The Passing of the Alaskeros." *International Examiner* (Seattle), April 1978.

———. "The Wapato Race Riot." *International Examiner* (Seattle), September 1979.

Interviews and Correspondence with the Author

Arditi, Rami. Seattle, 21 January 2011.

Catague, Emma. Seattle, 6 January 2011.

Della, David. Seattle, 28 December 2011.

Domingo, Kalayaan. Seattle, 23 August 2011.

Domingo, Ligaya. Seattle, 22 August 2011.

Domingo, Lynn. Seattle, 30 March 2011.

Doniego, Angel. Seattle, 2 July 2011.

Farinas, Dick and Rosita. Seattle, 9 September 2011.

Foz, John. Seattle, 16 December 2010.

Gurtiza, Rich. Seattle, 16 December 2010.

Hatten, John. Seattle, 9 March 2011.

Ikoma Ko, Elaine. Seattle, 1 September 2011.

Laranang, Julia. Seattle, 14 January 2011.

———. E-mail exchange with author, 13-26 September 2011.

Mast, Terri. Seattle, 12 December 2011.

Mensalvas, Chris. Selah, Wash., 30 June 2011.

Occena, Bruce. Seattle, 2 July 2011.

Pascua, Andy. Wapato, Wash., 1 July 2011.

Sugiyama, Alan. E-mail exchange with author, 7-18 September 2011.

Suson, Alonzo. Seattle, 2 July 2011.

Van Bronkhorst, Emily. Seattle, 28 December 2010.

Veloria, Velma. Seattle, 15 August 2011.

Viernes, Conan. Wapato, Wash., 1 July 2011.

Viernes, Stan. Wapato, Wash., 1 July 2011.

Viernes, Steve. Selah, Wash., 30 June 2011.

Woo, Michael. Seattle, 2 September 2011.

Websites

Alaska History & Cultural Studies

"Governing Alaska: Federal Influence in the Territory." http://www.akhistorycourse.org/articles/article.php?artID=137 (accessed 29 July 2011).

Carlos Bulosan Memorial Exhibit

"Chris Mensalvas." http://www.bulosan.org/html/organizers.html (accessed 18 November 2010).

"The Reform Movement of Local 37: The Work of Silme Domingo and Gene Viernes." http://www.bulosan.org/html/local_37.html (accessed 25 October 2010).

HistoryLink

David Wilma, "Automated salmon cleaning machine developed in Seattle in 1903." http://www.historylink.org/index.cfm?DisplayPage=output.cfm&file_id=2109 (accessed 24 July 2011).

Seattle Civil Rights & Labor History Project

Caughlan, John. Interview, 20 November 1998. Cindy Domingo Collection. http://depts.washington.edu/labpics/repository/d/13869-2/John-CaughlinInterview.pdf (accessed 12 December 2010).

Dade, Nicole. "The Murders of Virgil Duyungan and Aurelio Simon and the Filipino Cannery Workers' Union." http://depts.washington.edu/depress/cannery_workers_union_murders.shtml (accessed 16 July 2011).

Della, David. Interview, 18 March 2003. Cindy Domingo Collection. http://depts.washington.edu/labpics/repository/d/13857-2/DavidDellaInterview.pdf (accessed 12 December 2010).

———. Interview by Trevor Griffey and Lindsay Park, 8 November 2004. Seattle Civil Rights and Labor History Project. http://depts.washington.edu/civilr/della.htm (accessed 25 October 2010).

Domingo, Cindy. Interview by Michael Schulze-Oechtering Castenada and James Gregory, 9 August 2008. http://depts.washington.edu/civilr/cindy_domingo.htm (accessed 18 November 2010).

Domingo, Nemesio. Interview, 28 February 2003. Cindy Domingo Collection. http://depts.washington.edu/labpics/repository/d/13881-3/Nemesio-Interview.pdf (accessed 12 December 2010).

Ellison, Micah. "The Local 7/Local 37 Story: Filipino American Cannery Unionism in Seattle 1940–1959." http://depts.washington.edu/civilr/local_7.htm (accessed 25 October 2010).

Fresco, Crystal. "Cannery Workers' and Farm Laborers' Union 1933–39: Their Strength in Unity." http://depts.washington.edu/civilr/cwflu.htm (accessed 25 October 2010).

"Michael Woo and Silme Domingo Report on 1973 Observation Trip to Alaska Canneries." http://depts.washington.edu/labpics/repository/d/12042-2/domingo+and+woo+report.pdf (accessed 12 December 2010).

Pascua, Andy. Interview, 21 April 2003. Cindy Domingo Collection. http://depts.washington.edu/labpics/repository/d/13849-2/AndyPascuaInterview.pdf (accessed 12 December 2010).

"Proposal to Form Alaska Cannery Workers Association, 1973." http://depts.washington.edu/labpics/repository/d/12034-2/ACWA+proposal.pdf (accessed 12 December 2010).

Woo, Michael. Interview, 17 October 2002. Cindy Domingo Collection. http://depts.washington.edu/labpics/repository/d/13877-2/MichaelWooInterview.pdf (accessed 12 December 2011).

Washington State Historical Society

Phillip B. C. Jones. "Revolution on a Dare: Edmund Smith and His Fish Butchering Machine." http://stories.washingtonhistory.org/leschi/teaching/pdfs/stsironchink.pdf (accessed 24 July 2011).

Manuscript Collections

Emily Van Bronkhorst Personal Collection

"KDP Statement." Gene Viernes Memorial, 1981.

"Referendum to Recall Constantine (Tony) Baruso." Flyer, 1981.

"RFC Election Slate." Flyer, 1980.

Janet Horne. "Victim's Last Words Stressed to Jury at Cannery-Union Trial." News clipping, *Seattle Times*, n.d.

"Memorial for Gene Viernes." Program, 1981.

Terri Mast. "Untitled." Written account of murders and aftermath], n.d.

Van Bronkhorst, Emily. Deposition to the FBI, 6 July 1981.

———. Direct cross-examination at Guloy Trial. Transcript, n.d.

ILWU Archive, Inlandboatmen's Union, Seattle

Bulosan, Carlos, ed. *1952 Yearbook: Cannery Workers Local 37*. Seattle: Local 7 ILWU, 1952.

"Local 37 Membership Meeting." *Alaskero News* (Seattle), April 1979.

"May 28 Mass Meeting." *Alaskero News* (Seattle), June 1980.

"Members Ratify 3-Year Contract." *Alaskero News* (Seattle), July 1984.

"Negotiations Update." *Alaskero News* (Seattle), June 1980.

"Our View on the '78 Election." *Alaskero News* (Seattle), March 1979.

"Report on Constitution Committee." *Alaskero News* (Seattle), April 1979.

"Viernes for Dispatcher." *Alaskero News* (Seattle), June 1980.

Ron Chew Personal Collection

Rank-and-File Committee. Election slate. Hand bill, 1979.

———. "A Fair Election." Hand bill, 1978.

Viernes, Gene. "Alaskeros." Unpublished manuscript, 1978.

———. Letter to Silme Domingo and Michael Woo, 1973.

Terri Mast Personal Collection

Domingo, Silme. Letter to Gene Viernes, 19 July 1978.

SPECIAL CREDITS

(for front matter, profiles, and unlabeled illustrations)